1

My Thoughts

By S.D. Owens

Thank you for purchasing this book and I hope you enjoy your read. Once you have finished I also encourage you to visit the web page; BooksBySDOwens.com to write a review. I look forward to hearing your views. Note; you may have to type the web address into the address bar to assure reaching the web page

I would also like to make note that for every book sold we will donate fifty cents to the American Alzheimer's Association

Self-Published 2015

Edited by; Sara L. Schwee

Cover art by; Anthony Williams

E book on Amazon kindle ASIN BO176PYML

MY THOUGHTS

By S. D. Owen

Dedication

This book is dedicated to two of my high school teachers that made the greatest impact on my life; Senior English teacher, Mr. Majesky, and Social Studies teacher, Mr. Stone.

Mr. Majesky, my senior English, teacher took me from a "D" student to a "B" student in English. He was a no nonsense teacher, that made all his students learn and earn their diploma. He had a reputation for flunking seniors. Little did I know at the time, his opening day presentation would have an effect on the rest of my life. On day one, he made it clear that each and every student was going to be responsible for their own grades. He would not cater to sports coaches, parents, or any other special interests, and if you did not deserve it, you did not pass. It was that simple. It was during this year that I learned how to believe in myself and trust that I was capable of being just as smart as I worked to be. Yes, I typed that correctly, as I worked to be. He did not just tell us to do things; he taught us how to do things. This man taught me that failure was the first step to success. However, I was the only one that was responsible for the number of successful steps I took once I took that first step.

Each person is responsible for their own success or failure.

Mr. Stone, on the other hand, was a type of teacher you see in movies or on TV. This man is responsible for teaching me to look at things from more than one angle. He is the teacher that opened my mind, gave me the ability to see past the obvious surface massage, and look for what might be hidden in the shadows.

I also want give all my fellow students at E.A.J. high in Mt Morris MI, props, I am proud to have graduated with you. Go Panthers!

Prelude

This book is an organized culmination of my thoughts on a few topics. Topics will range from my thoughts on politics, term limits, the pledge of allegiance, same sex marriage, religion, abortion and by all means immigration.

A little about me; I have never written a book and by all normal standards, I am not qualified to be an author. I was just the average student in high school and college. My grades in English and Writing classes were middle to average at best, that may show at times while you are reading this book. However, it is my non-formal education and life experiences that more than qualify me to write this book. I am just the average Joe here in the U.S. I am not rich or famous, I don't have a TV or radio talk show, and for the most part, I have accomplished nothing of significance in my life, safe one thing; I am a father that has raised seven successful children. I actually live in the real world of these United States of America and have raised a family of good law abiding citizens right in the midst of all the turmoil and drama. My views, points, and suggested fixes come from a person that has lived and is living right smack dab in the middle of the very points and issues we will be talking about.

Virtually every person that writes books on the topics I will be covering writes from what I call the "ideal world view," whereas I am writing from the "real world view." What I mean by this is that all the other authors, while good people I am sure, and all have good intentions with their books and ideas, are living in the upper class and are in the higher society of our country. I am sure that some actually lived in the middle class or even the lower class, but I am willing to bet that each and every one of them had advanced their socio-economic status greatly by the time they wrote their book(s). Therefore, even those were being written from memories of experiences. I, on the other hand, am writing my book while trying to figure out how I will pay next month's rent, pay my electric bill, put gas in my car, and figure out what I will have left for the dinner table. I am the person that has been on the food stamp program and have friends that still are, so I can speak first hand on what changes should be made as well as how they can be made. I am one of the people that can say The Affordable Healthcare Act, while flawed as it may be, is 100% responsible for saving my wife's life. Yes, the law forced us to get insurance that neither of us had, had for nearly 20 years because of budget restraints, hence neither of us had seen a doctor in all those years. The policy we got made it mandatory that we both see a doctor within 90 days. On my wife's first visit, the doctor found a rapidly growing cyst on her uterus. By the time the doctors could do the surgery my wife's uterus was 6 times the size it was supposed to be. There is no question she would not have made it another year.

So, I am not writing from the same perspective as other writers. So, who am I to be writing this book? Let me explain why I am both capable as well as qualified to write this book. As I said, I am just the average Joe living here in the U.S. I have been married four times; my first wife died from cancer, my second marriage ended in divorce, while my third wife was murdered, and my fourth wife is doing just fine. Two of my wives were white, while the other two were black. I have seven children, two biological and five step children, as well as five grandchildren. I was born and raised in Flint, Michigan in the 1960's and 1970's before graduating high school in 1980. I then landed a job that kept me moving around the Gulf Coast states for most of the 1980's. I finally settled in Louisville Kentucky, which I have happily called home for about 30 years. During this time, I have raised my children to be confident, educated, law abiding, productive members in our society. My two youngest stepchildren are still single but leading strong productive lives in the Kentuckyanna area. My middle three stepchildren are married and raising families in California and Texas. My oldest daughter and her husband are raising two children of their own in a small town in Louisiana. My oldest son and his wife are raising their two children in New Orleans, Louisiana. Furthermore, my oldest son is a United States Marine Corps veteran that served in Iraq and is currently a deputy sheriff in the New Orleans LA area.

Why did I choose the title to be "My Thoughts"?

We are always hearing Senator So-and-so, or Congressmen Johnny B. Goode or even Dr. Lovemuffin, telling us their thoughts on our societal issues and how we should think, feel, or behave. The problem is that none of these people are willing or able to say the true real things that are needed to be said, all of them are speaking from or about the "ideal world," a world that the vast majority of us know nothing about. They give us their thoughts and suggestions from way up on the pedestal of privilege, and by privilege, I do not mean white privilege, I mean socio-economical privilege. So I got to thinking, for as long as I can remember, I have had thoughts. We all have thoughts. For the most part I never felt people really cared much to hear my thoughts, so I always kept them to myself. It was not until my mid 30's when I got involved with the Justice System and the Department of Corrections that I began to realize that my thoughts not only made sense to me, but to others as well, and without question, became worth sharing. However, it has taken almost 20 more years of shaking my head in frustration over all the thoughts from all the pillars of privileged minds before I decided to take this step of sharing my thoughts openly.

I am willing to bet that every person that reads this book will agree whole heartedly with at least one section or point, while yet outraged with heated passion at my point(s) in another section. But, that is what I am looking for and let me tell you why. I am a person that does not have many true friends; to me, a true friend is a person that tells you what you need to hear, not what you want to hear. A true friend is a person that will tell you when you are wrong even when you are thinking you are right. (Balaam's donkey Num 22;22). I am one that if my friend is wrong, I will tell him, and if my enemy is right, I will acknowledge that. It is simple to me; right is right and wrong is wrong. There is no taking sides or riding with my friend just because he/she is my friend. No, again right is right and wrong is wrong. People now days want sides to be taken based on alliances and allegiance rather than on what is right or wrong. An example is our politics; the people running our country base all their votes on who wrote the bill, not on whether it is good for our country. Since I don't think that way, I don't have many friends. At the same time, I also have no enemies that I am aware of either, which also makes my credibility for writing this book all that much better.

Therefore, as a regular everyday Joe in this country that lives in the real world not on a pedestal of privilege, I decided it was time to share my thoughts. I am not ashamed to say I am proud to be an American, a low income class, marginally educated, deep in my religious principles, while working on the real streets of American and as a father of seven successful children, one that is a Marine that served in Iraq, I have a vested interest to share my thoughts.

Chapters

1.   Pledge of Allegiance   13

2.   Thanksgiving   22

3.   America's Conception   27

4.   Media   32

5.   Our Economy   40

6.   Politics   92

7.   My Thoughts on War   113

8.   Immigration   125

9.   Gun Control   141

10.   Climate Change   147

11.   Same-Sex Marriage   153

12.   Abortion   163

13.   Religion   169

14.   Closing   241

Chapter 1

The Pledge of Allegiance

I insist on starting with an issue that is dear to my heart, the Pledge of Allegiance. The Pledge of Allegiance is a key American political practice that has been sidelined by one of the very rights it was designed to give pride too. The First Amendment granting the right to religious freedoms is a right that is longed for by many peoples and nations the world over. However, in our land of the freedom of interpretation and application, it is this very right that is creating so much confusion, anxiety, hostility, hatred, and discrimination. On this issue of the pledge, there are a handful of people that do not feel comfortable with some of its wording. Thus, we have sidelined the practice of reciting our pledge of allegiance in schools and at other gatherings. However, it is neither this amendment nor the people that are applying it that are keeping the pledge out of practice. No, not at all. The ones that are keeping the pledge out of practice are our country's leaders. Yes, the very people that we have voted into office to make sure our country runs right are in all actuality the ones that are keeping the pledge on the sidelines.

The history of the pledge follows;

The original Pledge of Allegiance was written by Francis Bellamy. It was first given wide publicity through the official program of the National Public Schools Celebration of Columbus Day, which was printed in The Youth's Companion of September 8, 1892, and at the same time sent out in leaflet form to schools throughout the country. School children first recited the Pledge of Allegiance this way:

> "I pledge allegiance to my Flag and to the Republic for which it stands one Nation indivisible, with Liberty and Justice for all."

"The flag of the United States" replaced the words "my Flag" in 1923 because some foreign-born people might have in mind the flag of the country of their birth instead of the United States flag. A year later, "of America" was added after "United States."

No form of the Pledge received official recognition by Congress until June 22, 1942, when the Pledge was formally included in the U.S. Flag Code. The official name of The Pledge of Allegiance was adopted in 1945. The last change in language came on Flag Day 1954, when Congress passed a law, which added the words "under God" after "one nation."

Originally, the pledge was said with the right hand in the so-called "Bellamy Salute," with the right the arm extending out from the body. Once Hitler came to power in Europe, some Americans were concerned that this position of the arm and hand resembled the Nazi or Fascist salute. In 1942, Congress also established the current practice of rendering the pledge with the right hand over the heart.

The Flag Code specifies that any future changes to the pledge would have to be with the consent of the President. (Courtesy of; Citizens of a founded nation working towards our nation)

So we can see the pledge had not been a long term practice for our country at the time that it was discontinued. As well, from its time of penning, there have been changes and adjustments; one of those changes in fact is the very change that has sidelined it. What this shows is; that changes or adjustments to the pledge are not forbidden, thus rather than sideline the pledge let's make the adjustments needed to get it back into action.

With that being the case, I propose we make another change, a change that will allow us to bring this unifying practice back into active duty. My proposal can be worked by either changing the wording and simply taking the controversial words of "under God" out, thus taking us back to what was recited pre 1954. Or, we can change the controversial words to something that would be non-religious and yet still invoking the pride of being a country singled out from the rest. My proposed pledge is as follows;

"I pledge allegiance to the flag of the United States of America, and to the republic for which it stands, the greatest nation of them all, indivisible, with liberty and justice for all."

Now, if nothing else, we can all say we have started this book by reciting The Pledge of Allegiance. You see, these are simple solutions to a senseless conflict. This is a clear-cut example of what is at the root of many of the problems marring the progress of our nation. There is nothing wrong with our leaders standing up and saying it is okay to make this change. After all, the pledge is to focus our allegiance to the United States of America, not to God. It is this very allegiance to America that allows each person the ability to have a god of their choice.

This is an example of a practice that seems to be running rampant in our society right now.

We always see the wrongs in others, which we never see in ourselves

Our government leaders are laying the blame for the sidelining of the pledge on the ungodly people of our nation. While in reality these leaders are using this as an excuse to create another divide in the very people that the pledge says will be "indivisible." Our country is not losing our edge because we have some people that don't believe in God. We are losing our edge because we have become a people that don't believe in taking responsibility for our own actions in life.

When James Madison fought for the amendments to our Constitution, he created or established the practice of our government being open to accept change when it is in the best interest of the country as a whole, and thus giving the "people" the feeling of hope, purpose or the sense of having a "right." The Amendments were never meant to be used as weapons against the very people they were created to protect. In this case, our Congressmen and Senators are using the protections granted by the first amendment to shame the very people it was created to protect. When our leaders continue to point fingers at "the people" that use the amendments for their protection as the reason for failure, we have to change our leaders.

This is not the time to make the conclusion that I am either a conservative or a liberal; I claim neither. I claim only to be an American, an American that only wants what is best for America in the long run. In this case, what is best for America is for our elected officials to stop hiding behind the curtain of religion and make the simple changes to get the practice of reciting the pledge back into action. Have you noticed that our political leaders running for office, specifically our presidential candidates never recite the pledge before they participate in a debate? Why is that?

The Pledge of Allegiance is a better practice for our country without the "Under God" wording then it is with it. Presidential candidate Ben Carson said it best when he said we cannot have any religions that override our Constitution. When we recite the Pledge without the religious wording, we are reciting a pledge that embraces the heart of our country's roots. We have to remember that our country was conceived by a bunch of misfits and rejects from around the world, some with religious beliefs some without. With that truth, we have to respect how they all came together, worked through their differences to create a nation that came to be the envy of the world for its ability to create unity while allowing people to maintain their individuality. The neutral wording creates the strongest opportunity for the broadest and healthiest form of American patriotism. The neutral wording makes no reference to any race, any previous national origin, and no ties to religion or lack thereof. The neutral wording allows all people to feel ownership, pride and patriotism in America. The United States of America, my country, our country, is just as important, just as valued and just as loved by the non-religious citizens as it is to the religious ones and we have to believe and accept that there more than just a few Americans that are not believers in God. That is why we are One Nation, "indivisible with liberty and justice for all." Emphases on ALL.

I strongly believe that re-implementing the pledge into our American way of life, including but not being limited to reciting it every morning in our school system, public or private, would go a long way in reducing both racism as well as terrorism here in the U.S. A pledge that is true to our American roots of acceptance of all.

Let's keep in mind that the men and women that grew up prior to the insertion of the line "One Nation Under God" are considered to be the greatest generation of in our times. So what does that say for the importance of that line?

On a side note here, as I mentioned earlier I find it interesting that our politicians that are running for office specifically for the office of President do not recite the Pledge before any of their debates. I will add to that practice, that I have noticed that both political parties push for their candidates to agree to back whomever wins their parties primaries and becomes their party's nominee, no matter what their ideological differences may be. However, neither party carries that same attitude with them after the presidential election. I do not hear the political leaders of either party agreeing that after the election we will commit to backing whichever candidate wins. On the contrary, they actually do just the opposite. A prime example is the current healthcare act. The Republicans have spent the last eight years trying to stop it, or dismantle it. They have said all along that once there is a republican president the first thing they will do it repeal the healthcare reform act. But now as the 2016 election gets closer the wording has changed, what is now being said is; we will repeal and replace it with something that works. Well if these same politicians would have worked together from the start we would already have a system that worked.

When my son came home from his tour in Iraq and saw a magazine cover with President Obama's picture on it, that said – "We cannot let him win." He looked at me and said – "Dad how does that make any sense? Why would we want him to lose? If he loses we all lose? We may not agree with him, but we should never want him to lose. And this came from my son to who calls his Commander and Chief – George W. Bush.

Chapter 2

Saving Thanksgiving

Thanksgiving is an American Holiday that also exudes American pride and patriotism. Thanksgiving, to me, is our best and most important Holiday. While people can and do differ on their understanding of its origin, Thanksgiving is our only holiday that has no religious, political, or racial ties. It is a holiday that calls for people of all different backgrounds, political practices and religious beliefs to come together and give thanks; it is a true American holiday.

Yet, Thanksgiving is being pushed to the wayside in favor of Christmas shopping, not

Christmas itself, but for Christmas shopping. We all know "Black-Friday" and the weeks leading up to Christmas are the biggest days of the year for retail stores. For years, actually decades we have ingrained ourselves into the practice of having the Friday after Thanksgiving as the kick-off to the Christmas rush. However, with the coming of the 21st century and the cyber-age, it seems ethics and respect are things of the past, giving way to the acceptance of greed, selfishness, and impatience.

We all accept and understand that retail stores make the vast majority of their money during this rush to Christmas Day. We are now seeing stores starting the "Black Friday" sales earlier and earlier, but it is not to make more money. It is to be the "first store" to make the money, and this is where I have a problem. This is simply the retail version of "Keeping up with the Jones."

In 2014, retail stores and malls opened on Thanksgiving Day to get the big rush of customers. In the practice of doing this, they not only forced their employees to forfeit time with their families on Thanksgiving, they also took all the shoppers away from their families as well, ultimately nullifying the Thanksgiving holiday, this is all just to be the first store to get the first Christmas dollar. The funny thing here was; I went into two of the big retail stores on Friday, the normal Black Friday, and found no crowds at all. I was able to do my shopping and get through the checkout line with no stress; I had no problems at all. To make things even more shameful, the following Tuesday, the weekend sales were tallied and numbers released. They showed that there were no big sales gain for 2014 as compared to previous year's during the same "Black-Friday" weekend period. Thus the 2014 Thanksgiving Day high-jacking by the retail stores was completely unnecessary.

However, I do believe I have a solution that would actually help the stores make more money and let people, customers and employees, both have a great Thanksgiving family event too. The way to do this is to bring "Black Friday" to Wednesday. Push all the sales, push all the hype, open early and close late. Then everyone could be closed on Thanksgiving and re-open on Friday with "Black Friday 2.0". This would allow employees and customers alike to enjoy the Thanksgiving holiday while the stores have their sales. The benefits' of this plan would be:

1. As I have already mentioned, all people, customers and employees alike, would have the opportunity to spend Thanksgiving with their friends and or families.

2. Next, employees would still have an opportunity to keep their work hours. By this I mean; they could work the long hours on Wednesday, off on Thursday, and then back to the long holiday hours on Friday. In addition to those hours, employees that have no plans for the holiday would have an opportunity to pick up some hours by going in on Thursday to clean-up and restock.

3. Then, the customer would benefit by being able to get out on Wednesday, do their shopping benefit from the sales, and still be able to spend Thanksgiving as a holiday, either helping others or spending it with friends and or family. And while spending time with their friends and family, they can all exchange stories of their "Wednesday-Black-Friday" events, and get all ramped up to go back out again on Friday 2.0.

4. The stores, on the other hand, can also use this to be a big winner. This can be a marketing event of "Black-Friday on Wednesday" sell the heck out of stuff, then have a stock crew come in for a few hours on Thursday (keeping in mind that there are some people that don't have ties to Thanksgiving) to restock, and then come back with a "Black Friday 2.0" on the day after Thanksgiving. Again, with this plan, everyone is a winner.

These are just a couple thoughts on how we as a nation can keep the integrity of our great American Thanksgiving Holiday, a Holiday that is true to our American roots of acceptance of all, as well as being able to have our Christmas kick offs too.

Chapter 3

America's Conception

After opening with a chapter pushing for the rebirth of the Pledge of Allegiance, followed by chapter two of praising the importance of saving Thanksgiving from the jaws of economic greed, I think it is only fitting that chapter three be my defense of our nation's conception.

I have been hearing more and more people coming out with a charge that America is an illegitimate nation and we should be ashamed because we stole the land from the Native Americans. To me, this is appalling to hear from fellow Americans. I am not disputing that the Native Americans were living here long before people from the European continent came. However, for people to actually say that our country is illegitimate because of that it is unacceptable. I hear this from white people, black people, and ones that claim to be Native American as well. I understand that people have the right to say what they want, but that in itself adds to my frustration.

The first question I have to ask is, have any of the people that are thinking, feeling, and talking like this every studied world history? If these people would have paid attention in their world history class, they would have learned that there is not a single existing country that did not take the land from someone that was already established on it. There have been wars over land for as long as man has been man. To top all, if you are a religious person, you have to accept that the act of war by one group of people to take land from another is directed by God. So, if it was okay with God for people to conquer land from others, who are we to condemn the act?

Furthermore, the very fact that you exist is because America exists. As well, the fact that you live in this country, America, the first country in the history of the planet that gave people the right to say stuff like that without getting killed, tells me you have twisted thinking. This is one of those times where I get to say, just because you have a right does not mean you should abuse it. For people to argue, or condemn, the how's or whys America came to be, is like questioning or condemning your very existence.

Being Politically Correct

The era of political correctness is getting out of hand. This is one area that being politically correct is not in me. This is an area that I do not mind if I hurt someone's feelings. Why? This country has given people "rights" that were unheard of prior to our conception. So, when people say these things and then burn or stomp on the flag, I lose all empathy for their cause. They cling to the 1st amendment as a right that gives them the power to do and/or say these things. But the way I see it; when you protest the very existence of this country, then you are no longer protected by the rights this country gives you. I feel the same way when a person burns or stomps on the American Flag and then say that they have the right to do so. No, you don't! Once you burn or stomp on that Flag, you are denouncing your citizenship. Once you do that, you are no longer a citizen, and since you are no longer a citizen you no longer get to enjoy the rights that Flag represents.

As you might have gathered, I am very proud to be an American. And I am all for people using the 1st amendment to protest. In fact, I believe that is one of our greatest rights. My oldest son is a Marine vet and I am very proud of him, the following is a story from my life;

On my son's return from Iraq, he was greeted at the New York airport by a crowd of enthusiastic, patriotic supporters, and naturally this made him feel really good. However, a short distance later, he was greeted by a crowd of protesters, and this bothered him; it bothered him a lot. One day, a few years later, he brought this to me, we talked and I explained to him that the crowd of protesters, which he said was negative, should not bother you, rather, it should make you that much prouder of your duty. While yes, the supporters are wonderful and make you feel all good, warm, and appreciated, in reality, it is the protesters that show that you have done your job. It is those very protesters that should give you the greatest sense of pride. I went on to explain, the supporters are good, but anyone can go out and rally for the popular/government's position, but it takes a true Patriot to protest **against** the Government's position. No country before us would allow its people to protest against its government; we were the first to not only allow it, but promote it as being healthy for our Country.

I stand by this belief. However, I believe there is a big difference between vocal protests and the ones that stomp or burn the Flag. Like I said, to me, once you willfully and hatefully desecrate the Flag, you have denounced your citizenship. Once that is done, you are done, let me help you pack your bags because you have got to go!

Our country is a great country and all the people that live here have the potential to be great as well, but we have to stop using the freedom of our first amendment to divide us. Yes, we have the right to speak our minds, but that does not mean we should. The conception of this country came about much like all the other counties, the spilling of blood and guts. Our conception is not the problem; the problem is our reality. Our reality is that we would rather blame someone or something else for our lack of success, and on this issue, it is the very people that can't find a scapegoat for their failure so they are now blaming it on the country as a whole.

This is a time that we all need to be coming together; we need to rally with pride and dignity. We are all Americans, no matter your color or your back ground, we are all

"...indivisible..."

Chapter 4

The Media

In chapter one, I pointed out that I am neither a conservative nor a liberal. I am neither right nor left, and I am not a Democrat or a Republican. I find when people accept labels or allow themselves to be categorized into a group that has pre-set ideals; they limit their ability to see things objectively. When a person joins a group or groups that have a preset platform of ideals and agendas, they instantly lose sight of the big picture. When our elected officials do this, it prevents them from doing what is best for our country. This country became strong and great by melding conservative and liberal ideas together. To implement 100% conservative ways would not be healthy. To see an example of a country that is focused of conservative ideals, look at Iran. To implement 100% liberal plans, would be equally unhealthy; look at Denmark. I also feel very strongly that our current practice of dividing into groups and continuously pointing fingers will be devastating to any progress for our country.

However, when the TV news media shows get involved, things go to a whole new level. Every one of them picks sides. They are either a pro-Democrat cast or a pro-Republican cast, or as they say, right or left. Inevitably on every crew and on every show, they are not only pro right or left; they go out of their way to only promote the issues they want to talk about. Then, they actually complain that the "other show" is bias. What I see is what I call "Free market censorship." By free market censorship, I mean the free market news media programs choose sides on an issue(s), then willfully only promotes the view they have. To me, this is censorship. Granted, it is not the same censorship as we are told to hate when the government tells the news programs what to and what not to say. However, when a news program takes a news piece and only gives one side of the story, that is censorship. Granted, it is chosen censorship but it is censorship just the same. I love the free market society but I see an ethical conflict between banned government censorship and legal free market censorship. Honestly, I am not sure which is worse.

What I do see in this practice are the members of the news media all having the same reason for this practice, which is; personal gain. News programs stay in business by having high ratings. When a show has high ratings, they can sell more commercials at higher billing rates. When these rates are high, the news host can demand a higher salary. Thus their main interest is not to **fully** inform the public but rather to get a bigger paycheck. Therefore, they are not really news programs; they are in reality entertainment programs. This is exactly where personal interest in subject matter provides them with their personal gains. These programs thrive off controversy; they make their living off conflict so they willfully choose to promote the topics they know will be controversial and create conflict. Furthermore, they are sure to direct the flow of or direction of their conversations on the topic to stay only on "their" view. This keeps the controversy going. Again, this promotes viewership and sells their commercials. So it turns out that it is in their best interest to make sure the finger pointing continues. Their interest has never been about doing what is best for our country, but rather, only what is best for their paycheck, hence their own personal gain. They are not finders of facts or seekers of the truth.

Here are a few of my favorite nighttime cable news show hosts and how I see them.

1. Hannity - Sean is probably my favorite one as far as humor goes. I give him credit for being very polished and great at what he does. I could never come close to being that good at what he does. However, Sean is, without question, the least

open minded of all the nighttime cable news hosts.

Sean always has his view and no matter what happens, he will never change it. The following is an example:

- On January 15 2015 the Hannity Show presented a young man that was involved in the McKinney, Texas aggressive police behavior. Sean's view was that a young man was trying to sneak up from behind the officer in an aggressive way.

- On this show, the young man that was seen in the video approaching the police officer gives his explanation of what had happened. He tells Sean to watch the video, which he would see that he was approaching from the front. As he was coming down a slight hill that was grassy, his foot slipped at the same time that his friend bumped into me, which is what caused me to appear to lunge towards the officer.

- Sean then proceeded to tell the young man that he was wrong, and that in fact was not how it happened.

This is vintage Sean, he is never wrong, and I am not saying he is. What I am saying is this is not news and it is definitely not healthy for our country when it is presented this way. This type of practice creates a stronger mindset into people that have the "I am not wrong" and everything is always "someone else's fault." mentality. (I have another book coming on this very subject) Our country is suffering right now from the "it's not my fault" syndrome, as I call it. When someone in Sean's position takes the stand every night, and says that his view is always right, and that there is no room for conversation, it has an effect on people. The people that watch his show on a regular basis end up picking up the same practice. The practice of – "Even with evidence and testimony presented to me that is clearly contrary to my current belief, I still maintain I am right."

This is not a healthy practice for our country

- Sean is also very good at having a guest on his show that has an opposing view, but never lets the person speak.

Like I said, if it's not Sean's view, it's wrong.

2. Megyn Kelly; of the Kelly files. Megyn is not far behind Sean in the "not too open minded" category, but I will give her some credit for

allowing her guests to talk and have good open conversation even when they have opposing views.

3. Bill O'Reilly; as for Bill, I have to say he is the most open minded and fair one of the Fox News bunch. My only beef with Bill is when he went on his rant about Beyonce not being a good role model for young girls. His rant was based on a music video she made that showed her in the back seat of a limo in a sexually suggestive and compromising way. All I can say is, Bill, I know you grew up watching Happy Days with Fonzie, as well as Porky's and Porky's revenge just to name a few. Bill, if we were to blame celebrity "suggestiveity" for people's bad behavior, we would have to be looking at you as "The Groomer of Assassins" because each one of your books is killing an important figure. Bill entertainers are not the problem, parenting in the home is. (I have another book coming on this very subject)

These are but a few of the nightly news programs that are helping to shape the direction our country is headed. I realize that is a sad and scary thing to say, yet it is the truth. Millions of people watch these and other news programs thinking they are "The news" when in reality they are nothing more the entertainment programs. Judging by the growing, hard-minded split in our county's views in the last 30 years, I have to think many people are using these programs as their only source for news. The birth of cable news programing has brought a whole different way to get your news. I will give it credit though, it is much more fun and entertaining to watch the current cable news programs than it was to read Time or U.S. News and World Report, but it is not nearly as reliable or trustworthy.

Our current day cable news media is just too polarizing. The free market choice to censor simply because they have the freedom of speech does not make it right. News, whether it is presented by a government agency or a free market agency, should always strive to be truthful, complete, and transparent. The bad part about all this is that I do have to concede that "the people" do have a responsibility to seek out more than one source for their news information.

The irony on this issue is that it is these same programs that have presented shows that talk about Hollywood and other entertainers having negative impacts on our society. Yet, they don't see themselves carrying the same responsibility.

We often see faults in others that we fail to see in ourselves.

Chapter 5

Our Economy

No President can create jobs. The driving force in our modern economy is not Christmas, or any other holiday sales, nor is it the president. The item that drives our economy is fuel prices; every recession has a direct correlation with a drastic climb in gas/oil prices. Common sense can show why the oil companies are the ones that run our economy. The only way the economy runs is for people to spend money. Our economy is dependent on millions of people spending money on a regular basis. However, the key is to spend money in more than just one place. So, when the oil companies raise the price of gas at the pump, they crush the economy. The higher the price of gas, the less discretionary dollars the spenders have. Most people have to live on a budget, and in a growing number of cases the budgets have little to no room for price increases. People have to prioritize their money; housing has to be first, utilities have to come second and then there is the food budget. In a lot of homes, this is the extent of the priorities, not because people are bad at budgeting, but because that is when the money runs out. So, when gas prices go up, some people have to decide which one of the three items in the budget gets cut.

For others, the problem is not much better. There is a segment of population that has a little more money and can have room for a fourth or even a fifth category in their budget, but the majority of them are a gas price hike away from being dropped down to a three category home. In all households, the scenario is the same, and in every case, when gas prices go up, the only ones that win are the gas companies. When Mary has to spend more money on gas, she has less money to spend on everything else. This means sales drop at retail stores, grocery stores, restaurants and even the very convenient store you buy your gas at. All this has a rippling effect. When people spend less money at stores and restaurants, the places are forced to cut the hours of their workers, which means the workers now have less money to spend and the cycle continues. The oil companies announce that they have record profits. This is exactly what I am talking about. When the oil companies lower their prices, people end up with more money to spend at other stores and low and behold, the economy is growing again.

No president or congressmen has control over this; it is all at the whims of the oils companies.

The interesting thing about our economy is that in every day and age, we think the economy is bad. In the 1940's it was bad, we strived to get better. In the 1950's it was bad, we worked hard to make it better. In the 1970's it was bad.... In the 1980's... In the 1990's.... and now, here we are in the 21st century and living better than ever and we are still complaining about the economy. The biggest thing about the economy and how we see it; is all in our perception of things. Granted, we were having faster or greater percentages of economic growth, based on governmental tracking numbers back in the 1950's, 1960's and 1970's, but we must keep in mind that our economy was much smaller at that time. Thus it was easier to have larger percentages of growth. While in our present economy we may be having a small percentage of growth, we are in fact still having a large actual growth. More importantly, it is better to have slow, manageable and progressive growth that is sustainable than it is to have large, fast and out of control growth that cannot be sustained.

Something that has to be acknowledged is; our country as a whole has changed our perceptions and expectations of what our responsibilities or living conditions in life are. For example, in the 1960's and 1970's, a minimum wage job was never considered as being a career. It was never looked at or expected to be a living wage or a sole source of income that was going to allow a person to live, much less build a retirement. Minimum wage jobs were stepping stones for people; they were jobs to help young high school and/or college kids have a little spending money without having to ask or depend on mom or dad. They were added supplemental incomes for the house when the main bread winner was not bringing in enough, or families just wanted a little extra money. There was a time back in the day when there was only one breadwinner; we only had one car, one TV, air conditioning if you were really doing well. Then, the goodies from the technology era started to hit the market. Once the 1980's came around, the days of the one breadwinner household became history. Households were in need of a supplemental income. The concept of keeping up with the Jones now became an expensive practice. Then came the 1990's. It turned into a two bread winner household society in order to maintain the increasing standard of material living.

The reason for this is because we changed the definition of getting by. Our lifestyle as a people changed, our standards as a society changed. We now have so much more "Material stuff" than we did back in the 1960's. Thus, it takes more money to live now. We have also changed our mindset of what a job is and what should have higher pay levels. Here are two examples; in the 1940's-1970's professional athletes' were middle class incomes at best. In fact, most of them had to work second jobs in order to make ends meet. Now, a professional athlete at the minimum rate is paid more than our president. When we pay a guy in the area of $10 million per season just to play a game, and his back up, or bench warmer, is getting a half a million dollars per year, we have changed our mindset or priorities. School teachers used to be held in high regards and respected; now teachers are laughed at by the very students they are expected to teach, all while parents defend the disruptive student. It's no wonder we are pushing to make the "minimum wage" a "Living wage." My question and or concern when we do this is, where is the incentive for people to get better? If all you have to do is get a minimum wage job, what is the incentive to go to college? When we set the standard that a burger flipper at a fast food joint gets paid the same as a doctor, we better be ok when we get the same type of service from the doctor as we do at the burger .joint

Our Economic Political Stress

With people in our society pushing for minimum wage to be a living wage, this tells me that a growing number of people are willing to settle for being poor. This action is developing what I call "The Economic Political Stress" that I see in our country. I coin this term from what I see as the building differences between the higher income people and lower income people. The lower income people continue to work every day and at the end of the week, month, and year, they have nothing to show for it. They have no material possessions, no savings account and no reason to think it will get any better, yet they continue to work. I see some of my friends struggling to make ends meet all the while stressing over what big government policy might change, and how that change will affect them. One of the biggest examples is Social Security; our low and midrange income workers get stressed every time the news talks about changes to the social security program. These are people that work hard every day, pay their taxes, which include the social security tax, and believe in our country to a fault. Yet, they keep hearing from the elected government personnel that everything they were working for and saving for through their payroll deductions is going to be taken away. What kind of hope does that give a person working in the lower income class?

Another example is the affordable healthcare act; this act was touted as being something that was going to help the lower income Americans, as it turned out, it is hurting far more people than it helped. While it has helped many, the truth is, it is not affordable. It does help those people that have little to no income. However, for the many of the middle income people, the cost for monthly premiums many have to pay, is just way to high; this affordable program is driving more and more middle income people into the lower income status when it comes down to "usable income dollars."

On the other hand, I hear some of my friends that are on the higher end of the economic scale complaining about how the government is doing too much for the poor, and that we are becoming a socialist country. Again I will use the Affordable healthcare act as an example; I hear this talked about as if it is the worst thing that could ever happen to our country. I hear it said that "we are a capitalist society and people need to take care of themselves, and that it is not the government's responsibility to use my tax dollars to pay for someone else's healthcare". While on the surface this argument sounds legitimate but in reality the "AHCA" will turn out to be one of the best things for the long term success of America.

This is why I call this "Economic Political Stress." Both high income and low income households are being affected by the political agenda of our time and stressing over it, just from different angles. With the Federal budget deficits so high and the 24 hour media, the working poor are constantly bombarded with fear that their small portion of the American dream that they invested in, will be lost by legislation or policy. While at the same time the working wealthy (and the not so working wealthy) are constantly bombarded with the fear that they are not getting a proportionate return from their taxes.

However, this does not have to be; we do not have to have this economic political stress. I will lay out how our Clash of Economies in this country has actually been a mutually benefiting factor for years. Yes, for scores of years, we have been working two different economic systems together, each helping to make our country stronger. We have had our capitalist economic system that has been thriving in part because of the social plans that our government has been implementing. Yes, I said that right. I will show how our capitalist economy is as strong as it is because of the socialist type of programs our government started implementing back in the 1930's. It also has to be acknowledged that the social programs could not have worked had it not been for our strong capitalist economy.

The Socialization of the U.S.

One of our most popular presidents of modern time once gave a speech that included the following words,

"Not a choice of right or left but rather up or down" *Ronald Reagan October 27, 1964.*

I have heard so much grumbling about our country becoming a socialist style government. In true terms of a "Socialist" we are not, we are though it seems trying to create a new economic style, a "Social Equality Economic System"; one in which some of the population work and the rest just live life. I say this because in a true socialist economy, the people actually have to work in order to get the social benefits. (Exceptions to the rule) While here, we are creating a system in which a growing portion of the population doesn't even have to work a day in order to benefit from the social programs, while another portion of the population work their tails off and end up struggling to live paycheck to paycheck.

This is to me the biggest area that has to be corrected. Then, there is another portion that do work but have more benefits than any of the other two portions combined.

It is concerning to me when I hear the wealthier people talk about this "socialization" and find what social programs they are upset over. It seems without exception the complaints are with the programs that cater to the elderly and the poor. On this, I have several thoughts and my thoughts are split. First, it is a resounding, Yes! We are, (in one area) leaning too far to the "Social benefits" vs the economic growth return. That area is the WIC, Section 8, and the Food stamp program. However, each of these programs in their current forms are not assistance programs but rather dependency traps. Yet, I never hear people from this same group complaining about the street sweepers, mosquito control or police protection. Each of these services, as well as hundreds of others, are just as "socialized" as the previous, the only difference is the direct or indirect effect the program has on the concerned community.

Our Constitution does not stipulate any type of economic system that we will be using. From the beginning we have used the capitalist system because of the relatively small number of people involved at the time and the lack of government size, experience, and responsibility. As time passed, our country and government evolved, the number of people increased exponentially, thus the governments' responsibilities changed/increased. Over time our population has changed; we have become increasingly more educated, more socialized and more humane. In turn, our government has grown in size, gained experience and took on more and more responsibilities. Since the Great Depression of the 1930's, our governments' responsibilities/policies have shifted to a socialized direction. However, our private sector economic system has stayed with the same capitalist goals. It is because of this split in directions that we have developed what seems to be such a disparaging split in upper and lower class incomes here in the U.S., while I maintain that it is this very split that has kept our income levels as close as they are. If we were to have maintained a pure capitalist system, the gap between the rich and the poor would be much greater and there would be little to no middle class.

Let me first address the frequently used opinion that "The welfare program is (has been) producing generations of people that have no work ethic because everything is given to them by the government." In theory this makes sense, but in actuality it is false. The 44th President of the United States was a product of this system. Whether you like him or not, whether you agree with him or not, you cannot deny he accomplished his academics by himself and He, and He alone works(ed) the hours it takes to be our Commander in Chief. That cannot be done by anyone without a heck of a work ethic. He is to name just one.

However, this stereotype statement clearly looks over another segment of our society that falls into the very same criteria of no work ethic, and that being the generation(s) of the well to do Americans. The children of parents that have made a lot of money and have no work ethic either; they are just like the "welfare generations," but instead of the government giving them the hand outs, it is their parents or grandparents. If it is true that the generations of welfare don't work because it will cost them their benefits, then it is also true that children of wealthy parents won't work because it is beneath them. Which is worse?

Our government has developed hundreds of social programs. Some are a humanitarian necessity, some are needed, some are good, some need some tweaking, and some are just a down right waist.

The humanitarian programs, such as helping the disabled and elderly are a necessity and none of us should have an issue with them. Though I have heard the argument that if we were not funding them, our population would not be as high and therefore no money would be needed for these programs. This is a cold view.

One program that I feel is a needed program is the Social Security Retirement benefits program. I say this because, there are companies that do not pay enough money for their workers to save, nor do they offer a retirement plan/program. The Social Security retirement program is good social program. This program is one that the worker has to pay into. Granted it is on a generation shift differential but the point is, it is not a free benefit program. Moreover, the Social Security program is far more beneficial to our country than just supplying a worker's retirement savings account. This program, which was a strongly contested program back in the 1930's, is arguably single handedly responsible for giving more people a reason to live than any other program in U.S. history. This program gave all the people in our country, then as well as now, a belief that there was going to be at least a small pot of gold for them just before they got to the end of their rainbow.

So the social security program is a good program with both good intent and good results.

In comparison, the food stamp program is a completely free program. The social security retirement program is in my opinion by far the best social program our government has taken on. This is a program that actually gives incentive for lower income people to continue to work. In fact, the more you work, the more you save. It is clear that the social security program is a social program that gives workers the incentive to work, work, work. Without this social security retirement program, lower income workers would actually do better for themselves by not working and simply being on the food stamp program. I say this because, most people want to work, and most people feel better about themselves when they have a job. But all people want to know they are working for a reason/goal, other than just paying the bills for this week or next month. All people want to know or feel that they will be able to retire and have some years to relax before the end of life. They all know it's not going to be a retirement of glory and world travel, but it will be at least some time to relax. With the social security retirement plan, this gives the people that are working the lower paying jobs that comfort, that belief that one day, they too will be able to relax and enjoy just a few years of retirement before it is all over.

Granted, the social security retirement funds are being stretched and are projected to run out in the foreseeable future. Therefore, the elected officials of our era, the same ones that don't care if/when we are TRILIONS of dollars over spent as a whole, are crying that social security needs to be replaced because it will run out of money in 20 something years. OH BOY. When our elected officials start publicizing this rhetoric, it is actually counterproductive to the workforce. When we have a workforce that is diligently going to work daily, and busting their tails for the little wages they make, but steady clinging to the hopes and dreams of one day, relaxing with their little social security retirement plan, that they have been steadily paying into out of every paycheck for years on end, and then these workers hear that all that they have been working for was a lie. This is so counterproductive, this causes the people that are and/or will be working these jobs to re-evaluate whether they should continue to work at all.

Here is a simple comparison, when "Enron," a private company, had all their top executives making huge amounts of money and then went under and took all the employees retirement savings with them. It was a shock to our financial mindset; it devastated hundreds, maybe thousands, of people. The government stepped in and said that this was criminal behavior. Yet, here we are with that same government, and our top executives (elected officials) are making huge amounts of money. We are in a huge financial deficit and they are telling the people that paid into their retirement that there will be nothing for them. I have to ask, how is this different? Why is this not considered the same type of criminal behavior?

The mind set of our elected officials 60+ years ago was that of hope, that of promise. They set the tone for the people of America to believe that the future was always going to be good. Furthermore, by developing and implementing this social security act, they gave our people something that was tangible for their future. This program gave each and every person a reason to look forward to their senior years. Our present day elected officials are taking all that away.

We need to fix the problem. Does anything else need to be said?

Let me elaborate. When I say fix the problem, what I mean is to really fix the problem. That does not mean eliminate the program, it means fix. There are ways this program can be fixed. One is to raise the retirement age; two is raise the social security tax, or three a combination of both, or four, stop dipping into the funds to use on other pork-barrel projects. Here is another idea, stop giving so much foreign aid and shift some of that money back to help our American seniors. I am sure there are a lot of people out there that can come up with other ideas. My only thing is, don't make it so complicated. Use the "KISS" system – "KEEP IT SIMPLE STUPID." First and foremost, we must have our elected officials presenting positive plans for the future. Our current mindset of gloom and doom has got to go!!

The Food Stamp Program

Food stamps, while a good idea in principal, is a program that needs to be rethought. When they first brought this program out in the 1930's, you had to buy them. You paid fifty cents on the dollar for them. Now they have become a gift, a way of life. A child can now grow up, move out of their parent/guardian's home, and be eligible for food stamps, never having to work a day in their life. Add, if this is a woman, she can get pregnant and now be eligible for housing and medical benefits as well. All this and she has never worked at any job, never paid a dime in taxes. Yet, the man/woman working and paying into the social security retirement program stress that once they get to the retirement age, there won't be any retirement funds for them. This just isn't right.

What if there was a requirement that recipients HAD to have worked, HAD to have had a job of some sort, or at the least be in collage to be eligible for these food stamps? It should be that a person can't simply turn 18 and be eligible. A person needs to have had a job and paid something in taxes before they can get any social benefits. This requirement works for the unemployment benefits, and social security, so let it also work for the food stamps. However, don't make it to where just because a person has a job, they get their benefits cut off. There should be an incentive to work; there needs to be a graduated program. By this I mean that if a person is working, they are now in a sense paying for the food stamps, so don't cut them off or even reduce the food stamps until they make an ACTUAL LIVING wage. Right now, our system is set so that a person is penalized if they get a job and make a certain amount of money each month. That threshold is too low and this should be raised. A family working making about $2000.00 gross per month and trying to raise children are realistically starving; that is reality. I know the people sitting on the television talk/news shows are saying that the people on food stamps are killing our country, but that is not true. It is the way the program is set up that is doing the killing.

This is a prime example of my point that not everybody lives in the ideal world. There is a large portion of our population that in reality will never be able to get a job that pays enough money to LIVE on, which is just reality. There is an even larger portion of people that will have to have a two income household and still not make as much money as the TV news/talk show hosts make, and yet, they have the audacity to point fingers and criticize the poor and low income people of America. My household can relate to this; we are a two income household and still don't equal an auto worker's income, let alone a TV personality.

Furthermore, when elected officials that are making $174,000.00 per year, plus a benefit package, and a comfortable retirement plan (all paid for from the tax base), are deciding that the food stamp program is too expensive and needs to be cut back, I have to wonder. The reason I have to wonder is because to me, the ethical numbers just don't add up. This is what I am talking about.

The numbers break down like this

A household of one person can make a maximum income of $1245 per month, and this equates to $14,940.00 per year. If you make less than that amount, you will be allowed to receive a pro-rated amount of food stamps not to exceed $200.00. So we have a group of individuals (535 congressmen/women) each receiving $14,500 per month (equal to the food stamp recipient's yearly income) of tax payer dollars saying we have to cut the $200.00 a month food stamp allotment from a person that only makes $1,244.00 a month. At this rate, the low income person will have to save his food stamps for 6 years in order to get as much tax payer dollars as the congressmen gets in one month. This is where my real world views differ from those of the people that live in the "Ideal world", from my view of looking at this from the bottom (real world) up,

I think our priorities are a little out of focus.

This is where I have a problem, and I am not the person that is on the band wagon calling for redistribution of the wealth. Oh no, not at all. I am a firm believer in the capitalist system; however, we are not in that area here. An elected official is not earning his/her money as a person in the capitalist way. These people are receiving their money from taxes, and thus, they are the very people that are taking the money from the rich/wealthy and giving it to themselves. Our elected officials, based on the way I look at the flow of our system, are the biggest welfare cheats in the history of any country. Some of my friends say we are going to a socialist state, but I say we are moving to a monarchy. If you look, you will see the same people/families are in Washington generation after generation, and what they do is tax the people (peasants) and they give it to themselves in the form of a paycheck. Then, they (Lords) get upset if somebody wants or needs some of it back.

Let's go back to the food stamp allotment and break this down. When I am finished with this break down, I will then present another plan to you, going much along the Reagan's trickle down economic stimulus plan that everyone loved so much.

Ok, a person receives $1245 in income per month;

1. The average rent in Louisville KY is $922.00,
2. The average rent in Detroit MI $793.00
3. The average rent in Dallas it is $1249.00 (Well if you live in Dallas you are already out of money).

I will work with the Louisville KY numbers; a person makes $1,245.00 per month

1. They have a rent of $700.00
2. Electric bill of $100.00
3. Water bill of $50
4. This leaves them with $395.00 for the month on "Other" things.
    a. We have to keep in mind in today's world if a person is going to be able to be or become successful a cell phone and at least internet connection are needed.
    b. Cell phones bill run about $50.00
    c. Internet service is about $50.00
    d. We are now down to $295.00 per month to budget.
    e. What about transportation? A person needs transportation in order to get to and from work not to mention other places. Let's say they take the bus; that is about $4.00 per day five days a week just to get to and from their job, total $20.00 per week $85.00 per month.
    f. We are now down to a budget of $210.00 per month.

g. This person will need to buy cleaning supplies such as soap, toothpaste, mouthwash, toilet tissue, dish soap, laundry soaps not to mention having a clothes purchase. Let's figure the personal needs area runs $50.00 per month and trust me that is cutting it cheap,

h. This person is now down to $160.00 per month to live on.

And we are saying $200 per month in food stamps is too much.

I think our priorities are a little out of focus.

These numbers are real, and the problems are real. If this person were to get sick with a simple cold and have to buy any medications, whether it be an aspirin, Tylenol or worse, any cold medications, they would be done. What if their rent goes up? What if the electric and/or water goes up?

I understand it is easy to say that people that are in this situation need to get better jobs. But, here is the problem; people that are living like this cannot get better jobs. In order to have a better job, a person needs better clothes, better transportation, and a better education. I will let you do the math, as you can see there is no money in the budget to get better clothes, better transportation, let alone a better education.

Yet our congressmen making $174,000.00 a year or $14,500.00 a month of tax payer's money (Reminder: this is more in one month than the food stamp person makes in a year) want to cut the food stamp allotments.

I pointed out that these programs have good intentions, but due to the way they are set up and executed they end up being counterproductive. I say they are not assistance programs but rather socio-economical traps. They are set up with standards or conditions that ultimately trap the participant into the lower income level.

Here is a true real life account of a couple that is really close to my wife and me.

This couple is married and live in an apartment. They both work, and they were on the government food stamp assistance program. They received $356.00 a month in food stamps. She received a nineteen cent per hour raise and they lost all $365.00 a month in food stamps.

Here is the math;

1. A .19 cent per hour raise on a 40 hour a week job equals $7.60 a week or $32.30 in a 30 day month.
2. So a $32.30 increase in GROSS monthly pay cost the couple $365.00 a month in food stamps.
3. So the couple ended up with a $32.30 raise that gave them a net loss of $332.70.

This is not an assistance program; this is a trap. An assistance program would not punish the participant for getting a small raise. An assistance program would be one that would constructively graduate its participants. I have a proposed graduation plan for the food stamp program that I feel would be much more beneficial to the long term economical health and stability of America.

My proposal:

If a person is allotted $200.00 a month for the first $1,500.00 a month ($18,000.00 a year) we then reduce it $25.00 a month for each additional $100.00 they make a month. This means that once a person is making $1,900.00 a month, they would get only $100.00 in food stamps, and at $2,300.00 a month ($27,600 per year) they would be on their own.

Or something like this;

For the couple above, when the household received the $32 extra, their food stamps would be reduced by $10.00 to $15.00. This graduated reduction process would continue until the stamp allotment was down to "0." The benefit of this gradual reduction process is three fold.

1. By reducing the food stamps in increments less than the amount of the raise you are giving the participants strong incentive to continue to increase the household income without penalty of loss. The reason I propose a gradual reduction rate at less than the amount of the raise is, because if the food stamps are reduced at the same rate as the raise you would in all reality be canceling out the raise. This type of action is just as counterproductive has having a net loss due to stamp reduction.

2. At some point with this reduction plan, the participant will actually be paying for their own food stamps through their increased payroll taxes.

3. This plan would ultimately bring more workers into the workforce, thus increasing the tax base.

The positive in this plan is that it gives a person a chance to grow independence. Under our present plan, low income people are trapped in poverty. As I laid out earlier, in our present system, a person has no opportunity to become independent. The system cuts a person off cold turkey at such a low level that they are forced to stay in poverty. They are forced to stay at such a low income in order to get food stamps, because if they make over $1,250.00 per month they lose more in food stamps than they make in income. Thus, we have a system that is trapping people into poverty, while my plan would be a plan that assists people into independence. I do not look at this as a "redistribution" of wealth, but rather a plan to create financial independence for all.

Additional thoughts on this are short and simple; the person(s) that are receiving the benefits need to have some responsibilities as well. Furthermore the government as a whole has a responsibility to not only help its citizens at the immediate time of need, but to also prepare them to be better, stronger and more self-sufficient people for years to come. So in fact it is irresponsible for our government to allow people to be in any of these programs without having any form of responsibility or accountability from the participants themselves. The way I see it, is that if a person is getting a benefit, whether it is food stamps, financial assistance for dependent children, WIC voucher, housing assistance or any other form of governmental assistance, this is an equivalent to getting a paycheck from an employer.

In every form of economic system there is always a form of give and take when it comes to compensation. Every employer and every employee have some form of responsibility and accountability. In this case, the U.S. government is taking the form of the "employer" while the program recipient is taking the form of the "employee." Therefore, each one has to have a set responsibility and accountability for this system to successfully continue. In our present practices, the government is holding all the responsibility and accountability with these programs, save one, and that is to stay poor. I recommend that we change this; I recommend that we give more responsibilities to the recipients. In doing this, the government will be living up to its' responsibility to not only help in the time of need but will also be developing the recipients to be self-sufficient in the future. Here are some of the added responsibilities or conditions I propose should be added to the social assistance programs that we currently offer to the poor.

1. Must be able to speak English.
2. Must be a legal citizen.

3. Must be a high school graduate, (this would make a big change in the high school dropout rate)
4. Must have or have had a job and paid taxes.
5. Must be a student in college before they can be eligible for this program.
6. Must pass a drug test at the time of applying.
7. Must be able to take and pass additional random drug tests while participating in any assistance program.
8. Must be willing and able to attend any self-improvement classes that include but are not limited to; employment training, self-awareness classes, home and surroundings improvement classes as well as parenting responsibility classes.

And keep in mind I am giving these suggestions as a person who was once a food stamp recipient.

Other changes can be;

1. "Child limit," I know of some ladies that look at having babies as a way to get a raise. That can be worked with, say, a limit of three kids and then after that the benefits do not increase.

MEDICAL COVERAGE FOR ALL

I will not refer to this section as "Obama Care" because the program is titled "The Affordable Healthcare Act," but I will not refer to it as that either, simply because it is not affordable. So I will address this section as if it is a program that still needs to be developed.

Many people are so against this; they do not think it is right for the government to provide medical coverage for the people. I just covered that a person can get food stamps, housing, and medical coverage without ever working a day in their life if they work the system right. While at the same time, a person can be working a 40 hour a week job for years and can't get medical coverage. They simply can't afford it and neither can their employer, so what happens then? They end up having to use the hospital emergency room for their insurance plan. Then when the bill comes, they can't pay it so the hospital has to file against them. More often than, not the person can't/doesn't pay. While the hospital writes it off, they also file against the person's credit, now this person that can't afford health care because of his/her low employment, is now facing a bad credit score. Which now can prevent them from getting a better job that would allow them to have healthcare, this could also prevent them from being able to get a student loan, which now prevents them from going to college. End result is that they become a low income statistic forever.

Our present system of mandated "Affordable Healthcare" is anything but affordable. It did not have to be like this; Kentucky produced a system that was simple, easy, and sensible and most of all, affordable for all parties involved.

While I do give President Obama props for forcing a healthcare system to be adopted, I also chastise him for forcing a system that is counter to its intent, just to get a healthcare system passed. An affordable health insurance system has been needed in this country for some time. With all due respect, both of our political parties have been talking about it for over twenty years, but this is one of those issues that had been sidelined by political party greed. (Back to the mindset that parties are competitive and that having preset platforms is counterproductive to the betterment of America.) It is clear to me that each party wanted an insurance program; they just did not want it passed when their "Parties' President" was not in office. Therefore, I give President Obama credit for taking the stand on this and making it an issue that had to be dealt with. However, like I said, I do believe it has to be modified in order for this to work.

I know my idea will get laughed at, but I truly believe the national healthcare act should have been set up like this. First, it should be referred to as the "National (or affordable) Health Insurance Act. Next, all we had to do was expand the Medicaid/Medicare program to accommodate our population that was in need.

Picture this as a program:

- First, leave all businesses that have health insurance plans alone. Whether they are big or small businesses, if they have health insurance for their employees, leave them alone. Next, leave the private insurance plans alone, meaning; do not tell the companies what coverage they have to have in their plans.
- I am fine with mandating some changes on the insurance companies. For example, they can no longer use the "Pre-existing condition" clause, or that they can no longer have cap limits on any medical treatments. These are two issues that were rightfully addressed.

Now for the implementation/application of my plan. Individuals that do not have health insurance can apply to the Medicaid/Medicare office, decide what the income is, and set a monthly premium for their benefit plan. There could also be a new set up with the Medicaid/Medicare office for small businesses to apply. This simple expansion of our already established program would have provided coverage for all and left out all the drama.

I am sorry, maybe I am to simple minded, but can anybody explain to me how or why my plan would not have worked? Like I said "KISS," keep it simple stupid!

These are the biggest social programs, otherwise called welfare, or entitlements

We focus on these items as if they were the ultimate cause of our financial problems. However, I believe that with a couple changes, these programs can be real assistance programs that help rather than trap the participants and burden the populace. I maintain that there are other programs that we spend even more money on but are never even looked at as social or welfare programs, but they are.

Let's start with some of the federal jobs.

Right off the top, I have to ask us to look at the Elected Officials. How is being an elected official not a social program? Are they not all benefiting from a form of a social program? The whole function of their job is, by definition, a social function. It is these very elected officials that want to cut the budget deficit by reducing and/or eliminating social programs. Yet, they have no problem maintaining or even raising their own pay. They make enough money to have multiple homes and fancy vacations, but complain about the poor getting too many food stamps or retiring while still alive. Hum!

I think our priorities are a little out of focus.

I know this will bring about a lot of backlash, but let's look at the federal employees that handle all the "social programs." Just think, if it were not for all the "poor" people, none of these employees would have jobs. The payroll and benefit package for these workers is very high. While I agree that these jobs are needed, I do know that these jobs come with a "career paycheck and benefit package." I can only ask, if we cut the number of people on social programs, what would happen to these workers? Wouldn't they be out of a job? Would they not then need the very social programs they once monitored?

Aren't these elected officials and federal employees indirectly recipients of social/welfare benefits?

There are thousands of other government employees that are indirect welfare recipients as well. All of the people that work for, or at places that are only open because the business receives federal grant money. Some of these are museums, almost all public transportation systems, and government park and recreation workers. None of these operations generate enough money (if any) to maintain operations on their own. With each of these, the key to continued business operations is federal grant monies. Hence, all the workers in these operations and many others that operate mainly off federal grant money, are, in all actuality,

74

simply receiving welfare checks. There is one difference and that is that their individual paychecks and benefit packages are far greater than that of the person(s) that are currently receiving the social benefit (welfare) programs that are so appalling.

My Thoughts on the Parks System

One summer, my wife and I were visiting a friend; he lives in a beautiful tourist town. While there, he took us out for some site seeing where we were able to see the local festival and some impressive buffalo farms. Along the way, we stopped at a couple of scenic historical parks, all of which were clean and well kept, and none of which did we have to pay any admission fee(s). One that really struck my interest was a little port town from about 150 years ago that died out because it could not keep up with the other port cities that got bigger. The town was so well preserved that, I am willing to bet it looks better now than it did when it was alive. We stopped in one shop that boasted that it was just the same now as it was in its glory days. Then I questioned the air-conditioning system, the indoor restrooms, telephone and stand up cooler with the sliding glass doors being used to sell cold drinks. So much for the boasting of authenticity. I have to wonder, do other people notice those things? Hum!

All this got me to thinking, how is this all paid for? Answer: tax dollars. Yes, the tax payers are paying to keep this historical attraction/park operating. This then got me thinking about just who it was that visited/benefited from this park. I then looked at the cars that were parked in the parking area; all were in good repair and relatively new. This gave me a clue that the vast majority of people that visited, were at least of the middle class. This got me to have more thoughts on the budgeting priorities of our tax dollars.

We have no problem spending our tax dollars not only on the payroll for the workers in these park/recreational areas, but also for the maintenance and up keep for them. Yet, funding of social programs for the poor are scrutinized. After evaluating the looks of the tourists that were there and the cars they were driving, this made me think; is it because the very people that utilize these areas are not the poor? The middle and upper class are far more likely to have the discretionary income, making them the people that can utilize these parks and recreational areas. Therefore, since this social program concept is benefiting them, then use of tax dollars for it is justified! Hum! I think our priorities are a little out of focus.

My Thoughts on the Road System

Our road system in the United States is considered to be the best in the world, but how did it come to be? In the early 20th century, our roads were horrible. They got a bit better with the advancement of the automobile. However, it wasn't until the Eisenhower administration that serious change took place. It was at this time that the Interstate system was developed and built; this is when our country opened up. Our road system is without question the best infrastructure design in the world, but how did it happen? When you look back, you can see the road system has been paid for by government grants and programs. So, we enjoy the comfort and convenience of our road/highway system because of another "social concept."

Yes, the development of our roads and highways came about because our government fronted the money to make it better for all of the people; this is by practical definition a socialist act. But, the only complaint I hear about the roads is, they need to be maintained better. Hum

My thoughts on the Capitalist Programs

I have noticed that there are no governmental capitalist programs. Yes, that was meant in a joking way. There are, however, scores of men and women that have been elected to Federal Office after being "practicing capitalists," just to receive social paychecks. You have to wonder why. The answer is simple. To be a successful capitalist, you have to be willing to work 24 hours a day and 7 days a week to make your American dream into a reality. But, as an elected official, you can work at best 40 hours per week for six months, run the country trillions of dollars into debt, and still be assured of a paycheck. Now that sounds like a successful socialist. Hum, am I the only one that sees that the average Americans are getting frustrated at the wrong segment of our population?

I think our priorities are a little out of focus.

My Thoughts on How These Two Economic Systems have been Benefiting to Each Other for Decades

It seems that the argument "we are a capitalist country, not a socialist one" creates a fine line on when the government can or should step in to help. In the social programs of food stamps and healthcare, the argument is that the government is doing too much and these types of programs are financially destroying our country. However, the government funds going to support "grant supported businesses" are called funds that stimulate the economy; though they sure look to me as backdoor high paid welfare checks, but those are just my thoughts.

Then there is the dollars that are being spent on the government parks and road systems. These systems are interesting to me. If we were in a true capitalist society these operations would be forced to make money or close. Yes I do mean that, make money or close! Parks are nice but they serve no financially productive purpose. The goal for the parks and recreation department is to give people a place to get away from home, see something different, to relax and enjoy nature. Who is most likely to do that? The people of the middle and upper class, in other words the people with the money. In a true capitalist society, these parks would all be "Pay to play" services. Yes, free tourist sites are good, but are they? Would they still be tourist sites if people had to pay to visit them? To me it only makes sense. If people want to see a city that was abandoned 150 years ago then they can, but the operational and up keep costs should not be at the tax payers' expense if it means we abandon our programs for the needy.

I think our priorities are a little out of focus.

Like I stated, our road system is the best in the world, but it was almost all paid for by tax dollars. In a true capitalist system, there would be roads but they would have been paid for and maintained by a toll system. We have enjoyed the "Opening of America" by the Eisenhower administration, all at tax payers' expense. This road system connected small town America to anywhere you want to go America, but the cost was paid for by the government. This made it so everyone, no matter what your economic station was, could benefit from the roads. In a true capitalist system only the people with enough money would be able to use the road system. However, by President Eisenhower deciding that the government would create and pay for the system, as well, he set the tone for the future upkeep and maintenance. It has allowed the poor and lower class Americans the same equal access to travel, relocate, and seek new or better jobs as the wealthy. Though the poor did not pay in nearly as much in taxes as the middle and upper class, I don't hear anyone making a stink about the social concept that allowed for this system to develop. I am guessing that this is much like the park system concept. The reality is that there are more middle and upper class families that use the roads, so it is ok to spend tax dollars on them. If the poor somehow benefit, that is ok too.

My Thoughts on This Economic Relationship

While these two economic systems are vastly different in practice and concept, they can be melded together in a way that can benefit everyone. As I say this, I think of how we as a people here in America have been teaching this concept right from the start. We say we are a capitalist people, meaning; we are working hard to capitalize on each individual's efforts to ultimately become as wealthy or to become the best at what we do and financially benefit from that. While socialism by definition is not the programs our government has been implementing or practicing, it does still have the effect of sharing or equalizing, allowing the have-nots to be equal to the haves in some but not all ways.

We teach our children to "share" when they are young and then expect them to "capitalize" when they get older. (Such a confusing practice)

Two real life examples of this these two systems working together for the betterment of all is the very park and recreation system as well as the road system I previously talked about. As I pointed out, the development of the roads was done by a social concept and it helped all of the people. The system, while costly yes, ultimately paid for itself hundreds of times over. When this system connected small town America to anywhere you want to go America, it created an economic boom that can never be duplicated.

Our road system has been given so much credit for boosting the economy back in the 1960's that President Obama wanted to use the same concept as the heart of his stimulus package in 2009. The idea was good, but the practice was flawed. The 2009 stimulus package was spent to repair our current system, not increase it. The original road system opened up new territory to the people. It gave us ways to get from place to place that we did not have before; it made travel simpler and more convenient. The economic effect of the road system was that it allowed for more people to mingle with other towns. Thus, there needed to be more hotels/motels, more gas stations, more grocery stores, ECT. This meant more people were going to be needed to work at all these new places. More goods were going to be needed for deliveries, more trucks and more drivers, ECT. This meant there was more money in the economy so production went up in all areas, thus the economic boom. Here is where the flaw in President Obama's stimulus package lies. The package was targeted to give money to existing companies to do repairs to existing roads. The work was done quickly and the big money went into the hands of a few people that spent it on some low ticket personal stuff. It was not a plan for a long term fix.

Had this money been spent to increase the roads, not repair them, it would have been better spent. As it is, the money was spent, the work was done and there was no net long term gain. Had he designated this money to increasing the roads, such as connecting some interstates that are incomplete then the stimulus package would be creating long term economic growth, working like the Eisenhower plan did. For example, connecting I-69 from Indianapolis, Indiana to Evansville, Indiana would have created the opportunity to develop new business along this route, which means new jobs, more income, more taxes and the economy continues to grow long term. The same thing could have happened in southern Indiana and Louisville KY: I-265 needs to be connected and have a bridge built. If that were to take place, so many new job developments would open up. Again this means more jobs, more money, and more taxes being paid; the economy improves and the dollars spent on the road and bridge would be recouped.

In contrast to the normal road development practice, these two states are having to borrow the money to build the bridges and then install toll systems for the local residents to pay. This is projected to take 40 years to pay off. This is an example of how the capitalist system by itself can be a hindrance; the toll system will cause people to think twice about going over those bridges. This meaning the dollars that could be spent by people driving over these bridges and stopping at local shops in that area of new development will be diverted elsewhere, meaning a loss in tax revenue. This in fact, is in contrast to the Eisenhower plan, all of I-65, I-64 and I-71 were paid for with tax dollars, in a social program way, but now the connecting bridges are being paid for in a capitalist style, "pay as you go."

My thoughts, the money can be better spent! This is just a tip of how our capitalist and social systems can work together to help us as a whole, or can be used against each other and ultimately hurt us as a whole.

These two systems have also worked together in the parks and recreation department to help each other. The parks are taken care of through tax dollars, and are free to the public. This causes more people to want to travel and visit them. This in turn causes these travelers to have more money to spend at local businesses thus improving the economy which is increasing tax dollars and ultimately paying for themselves. Again, the two systems are working together for the betterment of the whole economic system.

How can the food stamp program work so that it is for the betterment of the whole economic system? In some degrees it already does.

1. By people receiving the food stamps we are enviably cutting down on crime. Yes there are some people that if the food stamps did not exist would get a job of some sort, but I can assure you there is a portion of the

population that would simply go rob or steal to get something to eat. Can the system be improved? Yes, but in the meantime the system is helping both sides.

2. The food stamp recipients have to spend the stamps somewhere. This means businesses are opening, that cater to those needs.

3. The government employees that are getting paid to handle the paperwork for the recipients are getting a paycheck, and in turn are spending their money somewhere.

If we were to implement a better assistance program similar to the plan I outlined earlier, there would be even more points to show how the food stamp program benefits the capitalist economy. Another way we can use the food stamp program to help the capitalist system that is under fire right now over the minimum wage amount.

1. If we revamp the food stamp program to work off a graduated reduction plan, we can use this to help the private sector with this minimum wage quandary. With the push for minimum wage to be increased to what is called a "living wage," the private sector employers are having a hard time being able to pay the increased wage.

2. The government assistance program can be adjusted to where it can work with the small business community so they can work together to pay the workers this living wage amount. It can be a cooperative system that the small businesses would pay their workers a regular rate and then turn in the time sheets on weekly or monthly basis. The government would then calculate the living wage adjustment and issue that in the form of food stamps.
   A. This would help the small businesses with their labor force and labor costs.
   B. This would help the citizens by having more spendable income.
   C. This would help the capitalist system by keeping people working, making more money, and therefore spending more money.
   D. This would ultimately help the tax base because ultimately, these workers will be paying for their own food stamps through their payroll deductions.

Again the social program(s) do end up supporting the capitalist system. Granted, the tax revenue return rate is small in this area, but it is better than no return at all.

Final Thought on This Subject

My point is, we cannot continue to isolate our focus of frustration of wasted tax dollars and blame the cause of the national debt on programs that help or benefit others (the poor), while at the same time being okay with or defending the wasted tax dollar programs that benefit the wealthier income brackets.

We always see the wrong in others, but never see the same wrong in ourselves

The most important thing here is, we all have to be more positive. We have to be willing to see all the ways that we as Americans, rich and poor alike, can benefit from both social plans and capitalist economic systems. What I mean here is that the capitalist economic system has been working for a couple of centuries now, but it was not until the last 60 or so years that more and more people have started to reap the benefits of this system. It was not until our government started some of the social programs in an attempt to help the poor that ultimately helped the capitalists as well. This has been overlooked by way too many for far too long. We are now at a point that we all have to come to grips with this. We all have to accept that these two systems have been benefiting from each other rather than hindering one or the other. In 1964, some guy named Ronald Raegan gave a speech that made real waives in politics. In that speech, he used the following words:

"You and I are told we must choose between a left or right, but I suggest there is no such thing as a left or right. There is only an up or down. Up to man's age-old dream – the maximum of individual freedom consistent with order – or down to the ant heap of totalitarianism."

I pose that this statement is a true statement still today, but I see it from a different view than others. I see it as; we do not need to continue the destructive path we are presently on of fighting between Liberal and Conservative politics, but rather see that these programs can and have been healthy for our country. It is clear that the present political practices are taking us in the "down" direction. However, if we work together, we will be choosing the "up" that Mr. Raegan referred to.

On more than one occasion, my friends and I have talked about the fact that the capitalistic economic system is not for everybody. The capitalistic system is a sink or swim system; a person is either successful or they are not, there is no in-between in this system. So, if we were to run both our economic system and our government policies on the capitalistic principals, we would have no room for humanity in our country.

I close out this chapter with this thought; if we are constantly talking about the religious/spiritual principals of the Founding Fathers as reasoning to support or repel specific governmental legislation (abortion for one); it befuddles me as to why the social programs are the ones that are being repelled. If we are going to use the religious/spiritual principals, who gets to make the call as to which principals we adhere to and which ones are "a waste of my money"?

When my son was very young, I explained the struggle for success in this country in this way;

Life is like climbing a mountain. Sometimes the climb is going up an easy slope and others it is a steep one. But the goal always remains the same; to get to the top.

With that said, we all need to understand that not everybody can be a John Rockefeller, Vanderbilt, Sam Walton or Bill Gates. Heck most people don't even want to be that wealthy. However, it must also be clear that there are some people that don't even want to be rich at all. There are some people that are just fine with retiring on a social security retirement plan, and there is nothing wrong with that. Some of us want to travel, some want to see the world, and are just fine never leaving their home town.

It's time to let go of our Economic Political Stress and look for positives on how the social programs will help the capitalist economy grow.

Chapter 6

Politics

The first thing I want to ask is when was America ever great? I ask that question not because I believe we were not, but because from the 1976 presidential election campaign, the non-incumbent candidate has always run with the slogan of "I am going to make America great again." It does not matter which party; if they were not the incumbent president, they ran with that slogan. If for forty years the candidates have been running with that slogan, I have to ask, when was America ever great?

That type of campaigning creates the subliminal mindset that we are not a great nation now, and that to me is not presidential. The person I want to see running for president is the person that see us as great but has aspirations to make us greater. We need presidents that lead with the attitude of "We are great, BUT..." The last president that carried that aura was President John F. Kennedy, who stated "Ask not what your country can do for you, but what you can do for your country."

My thoughts on politics will mainly focus on the structure and operation (or lack thereof) of our federal branches of government. Some 238 years ago, the United States of America was a new and experimental government. Time has shown this experiment has been rather successful. But, time has also shown us that we needed to make a few adjustments along the way. First, it took our founding fathers about 13 (March 4, 1789) years to get from the Declaration of Independence to the ratification of the Constitution in its final form. It was then, just less than a year after the ratifying of that Constitution, that it was realized changes were needed; thus the Bill of Rights was ratified two years later (1791). The Bill of Rights contained the first ten amendments. There were 17 more yet to come, with the most recent amendment ratification in 1992 (proposed in 1789, it only took a bit over 202 years to get ratified, but ratified it was). The point here is, that even though our Government was conceived, developed, created and finally implemented way back in the late 1700's, it has grown, and changed as it found the needs for change. As we found weak spots, we changed to make those spots stronger, and thus making our country stronger. This is why we, the people of the United States of America, can proudly say our Constitution is the oldest active constitution in operation in the world.

We are now, again at one of those times of change. Yes, it is now time for a change; time for a change that will be positive. A change, which without question has to be made, a change that is not unprecedented, and in principal was, applied once before. [The **Twenty-Second Amendment** (**PROPOSED MARCH 21, 1947; ADOPTED FEBRUARY 27, 1951**)]

With 27 amendments to our original constitution, and 6 of those amendments directly addressing changes in the way(s) we elect our federal officials, including putting term limits on the office of president, this leads me directly into my first and most important thought in this chapter.

TERM LIMITS

My thoughts are that since we have a limit on our president, then all others should be held to the same standard of term limits. I have several reasons for this position.

1. If our Commander In Chief, to whom is the leader of our country, the highest position, and for all accounts, the most powerful person in the world, is held to a limited amount of years in office, then it is only ethical common sense that

the people he/she will be leading are held to an equal standard.

2. When a person has no term limit it creates an inefficient system. I say this because;

   a. When a person knows they only have "X" amount of time (years) to get something done, they are much more apt to work toward the completion of that work.

   b. When a person has no limit, then the goal of getting re-elected becomes a higher priority than passing productive legislation, or doing your job!

   c. When people stay in office through multiple presidents, it sets the tone for partisan practices. I say this because, this allows people to get in their mind that if there is going to be some good legislation passed; they can block it until "their" president is in office. Then when "their" resident gets in, the other party plays tit for tat, and thus the "Do nothing congresses" never end.

3. Therefore, if everyone in the House of Representatives and the Senate could serve no more years, or terms than the president, they would be far less likely to spend their time blocking good legislation in an attempt to save it for "their president."

a. A term limit of 2 (Senate) and 4 (House of Representatives) would make it so our elected officials would no longer be burdened with having to focus on re-election all the time. With term limits, they would be freed up to only have to focus on what is best for our country, or doing their job!

4. Term limits would also cut the "pork" spending drastically. You can look at the Pork that is tagged to most of the legislation and see that it comes from the long term officials. This happens because of the long term "I scratch you, you scratch me" practice. If elected officials were held to eight years (House of Representatives) 12 years (Senate) max limits, this "scratching" practice would stop.

The following are some states that I say support my claim.

I will start with the history of the Senate.

- Of the 1,950 plus senators that have been voted into office, there have been 264 members that have served for a minimum of 18 years (3 term) [This as of the time of the writing of this book],

- Of those 264 senators, 126 have been in term since 1951, (ratification of 22nd amendment).

- In the first 62 years, there were 58 members that served for 18 years or longer (The longest being 35 years: William B Allison, Iowa 1873 – 1908).
- Then, in the next 50 years, we had but 80 members that served for 18 or more years, (The longest being 42 years by William Henry King of Utah 1917 – 1941).
- However, from 1951 thru 2013 (63 years) we have had 126 members that have served for at least 18 years, with fifteen more on the cusp by the 2020 senate elections.
- Forty-one (41) of them serving for at least 30 years or 5+ terms, the longest being 51 years (1959 to 2010.) by Senator Robert Byrd of W. Virginia. (Senator Byrd had an additional 6 years in the U.S. House (1953 - 1959).

Thus, in the Senate, we can see that the number of plus three terms senators more than doubled in the last one third of our congressional history. Granted some will say that this is a direct result of better health care and living conditions, thus a person lives longer. This would not be an acceptable explanation since it cannot apply to our president.

In the House of Representatives, which has but only a two year term;

- I find that of 44 of the top 50 longest serving members have served since the ratification of the 22nd amendment (1951).
- With having the longest in service member being an active member, Congressmen John Dingell of Michigan with time in of 59 years and counting. That means if we do the math on this, the people of Michigan have re-elected this man 29 times. Yes that is correct- 29 times.
- To make this even more astonishing, the second longest serving House of Representatives is also an active member from the state of Michigan with 49 years in and counting. That gives him 24 times that he was re-elected.
- Both of these men are representatives of the Detroit area in Michigan. Looking at the rate and time frame of decline for the city of Detroit, this should be proof enough that we need term limits.

Dingell was first elected in 1955 and Conyers in 1965. All of us can see the difference in Detroit today as to what it was back in the 50's and 60's. It is clear from the state of affairs in and around the Detroit area that neither of these two men have had any positive influence on the city. The people in that area have not been strong enough to see that a change was (has been) needed. So if the officials will not step aside and the people will not move them aside, then it is incumbent on our government that was created on the concept of "checks and balances" to pass an amendment mandating term limits to protect itself from just this sort of dysfunction. To further my point even more on this issue, Michigan has re-elected Senator Carl Levin to serve for 35 years.

Michigan is a state that has been in a steady decline for decades and it has only been getting worse. Again, I can't say this enough; this right here is a clear textbook example of the need for term limits. The elected officials ran on the premise that they would do what is best for their constituents and when it becomes clear that they are not doing that, and this is clear in the case of Michigan and Detroit in particular, then the elected members should step aside. However, if they can't see that they are not getting the job done, and don't willfully do the right thing by stepping aside and letting some fresh ideas step in, then the voters should replace them. Yes, this is how the system is supposed to work, but it is clear here with the situation in the Detroit area that even the voters can't always be counted on to do the right thing. Therefore, this is the clearest example of how the government needs to have checks and balances that will help to protect the people against this very situation.

This is just one example of how trusting and leaving some things without controls, restrictions or "limits" can go bad, and in this case it is really bad.

This is not just a Michigan, or Detroit problem. Detroit just happens to be the most blatant and obvious situation. I will now show that with 44 of the top 50 longest serving representatives in history have served in the last half century, and with five of these men serving for at least 50 years,

- Dingell, MI, 1955 - present,
- Jamie Whitten, MS 1941 – 1995,
- Carl Vinson, AZ, 1914-1965,
- Emanuel Celler, NY, 1923-1973,
- John Conyers, MI, 1965- present)
- And two are active rep's one at 59 years and the other at 50 years and counting.

While in the senate, 41 Senators have served for at least 30 years (5 terms) in this same time frame.   Ironically, the increased number of congressmen serving extended years in office (or terms re-elected) picks up just after the 22nd amendment (limiting the president to only two elected terms) was ratified (1951).

There is also yet another staggering correlation. The productivity and efficiency of congress begins to drop off from this point as well.

- 81st congress (1949-50) had 10,502 bills introduced with 2482 bills passed.
- 91st (1969-71) 21,437 introduced with 1130 passing
- 101st (1989-90) 6664 introduced with only 968 passing
- 111st (2009-10) 6677 bills introduced with 861 bills passing
- 112th (2011-2012) had 6845 bills introduced and only 561 passing

This lends credence to my claim that our elected officials are playing the "I will wait until my president is in office before I will try to pass any meaningful legislation" game. This list of congressional activity clearly shows that this has been a developing trend. This has not just been a factor in the last two administrations (43 and 44); this shows it is a building trend. The only common denominator is the growing number of congressional members that are getting re-elected to what I call "Emperors on the Down Low," the American

Monarchs. This is why I do not agree with those that say our elected officials are staying in office longer now, simply because of improved healthcare. I say that people are now staying in office longer because they can, and it is not because they want to do wonderful things for America, but rather because they are looking to benefit themselves. Whether it be because they want the salary and benefits or because they want their name in the record book as the person that lasted longer than the last person, I don't know, but I can tell you staying in office for more than eight years or two terms is not healthy for the productivity of America. Let's leave the "Ironman" awards to the athletes.

Therefore, my thoughts: No congressional elected official should be allowed to server more years or terms then the President. 4 terms or 8 years max for the house and 2 terms 12 years max for the Senate.

This can only be done by way of a constitutional amendment. Since the very people that we are asking to put these limits on would be responsible for bring this amendment legislation to a vote; it is not likely to happen. Therefore, I propose that there has to be a way to force this issue. It was not until the death of President F.D. Roosevelt in his 4th elected term that congress drafted the legislation for the 22nd amendment. Part of the argument at the time was;

Using the same fundamental arguments as history has used

> *"These men feared that if any man were to exceed two terms in office, it would give him the opportunity to become a despot, which is one of the things they were trying to avoid. They didn't want to leave too much power in the hands of single person." (Constitutional facts.com)*

Currently, we have 20 senators and 82 representatives that have been in office for more than 20 years. If this kind of long term political life was to happen in any other country, we would frown on it as being a type of Monarch or Dictatorship, and would be pushing them to be truer "Democracy." We don't look at ourselves like that because these offices are not that of the president, but we all know when these congressmen get in office for this amount of time they start wielding a lot more power. This is ridiculous, if these people were working in a capitalist workforce, there is no way they would be working that long. This clearly shows that term limits are required on all elected officials. If for no other reason than the one presented for limiting the

President, "*…to much power in the hands of a single person,*" and when a person is in office that long, Senate or House you develop power, a power that can be and has been detrimental to the long term health of **OUR** country.

We always see the wrong in others, but never see the same wrong in ourselves

So how do we get around this?

If the elected officials do not bring this to a vote on their own, the constitution does provide an answer. In article V of the constitution;

Article V

The Congress, whenever two thirds of both houses shall deem it necessary, shall propose amendments to this Constitution, or, on the application of the legislatures of two thirds of the several states, shall call a convention for proposing amendments, which, in either case, shall be valid to all intents and purposes, as part of this Constitution, when ratified by the legislatures of three fourths of the several states, or by conventions in three fourths thereof, as the one or the other mode of ratification may be proposed by the Congress; provided that no amendment which may be made prior to the year one thousand eight hundred and eight shall in any manner affect the first and fourth clauses in the ninth section of the first article; and that no state, without its consent, shall be deprived of its equal suffrage in the Senate.

So there is a solution if the Senate and House of Representatives don't do the right thing. The Constitution did give the people the power to protect themselves from a runaway government. The question, are we willing to act on this

My thoughts on elected officials' salary and benefits.

Along the same line as term limits, is the out of control salary and benefit packages our elected officials are giving themselves.

1. Any and all salary and benefits packages should be voted on in a national election.

2. When you leave office, your salary and benefits end.

    a. We have a government that is "By the people, for the people." When tax dollars are being spent on elected officials that are no longer in office that is not "for the people."

When our country is in debt as deep as we are, how in the world are we paying the very people that voted in budgets that put us in debt, even more money once they leave office? Is this no worse than the CEOs of companies that get paid fat bonuses when they leave a company after running it into the ground? On top of that, don't you find it classless, or better yet unethical, for any of our elected officials to even accept any "after service" benefits? Oh Boy!!

When you leave a job (Office) and the company (country) that is in financial disarray, you do not deserve any post-employment compensation. Moreover, **IF** there were term limits that make all elected offices equal to the president, as being 2 terms or 8 years, there would be no reason for post office benefits. Nobody gets benefits after 8 or even just 12 years on a job. Beside, these are people that by job definition were "public servants", not leeches.

Budget issues

First on this issue, I hear time after time people complain about this deficit issue and almost always use the analogy; we can't run our personal checkbook like this!! Well, that analogy is bunk! I say that because in fact, we as Americans do just that. We all spend over our budget, which is why the banks offer "overdraft protection" (I use this option myself). As well, we all have credit cards. So, we are all in a budget deficit situation to some extent, but agreed, not a trillion plus dollars!!!!

However, my thoughts on the Government budget is simple, there should be a mandatory **Balanced Budget**. With that not being in place, we as a country that prides ourselves as being a government that is protected by a system of checks and balances, needs that type of protection in this area. I say the word "protection" strongly, because it has become clear over the past five generations that our elected officials will not willfully balance the federal budget, and it has become clear that this continued rising deficit is a threat, if not the greatest threat to our very existences.

> **Note;** required reading for all elected officials should be President George Washington's' Farewell Address. In this

letter, he goes to an extreme to advise the importance of not, I mean NOT, having a budget deficit.

Every time our federal elected officials take office they are sworn in with the following oath;

> **DO YOU SOLEMNLY SWEAR THAT YOU WILL SUPPORT AND DEFEND THE CONSTITUTION OF THE UNITED STATES AGAINST ALL ENEMIES, FOREIGN AND DOMESTIC; THAT YOU WILL BEAR TRUE FAITH AND ALLEGIANCE TO THE SAME; THAT YOU TAKE THIS OBLIGATION FREELY, WITHOUT ANY MENTAL RESERVATION OR PURPOSE OF EVASION; AND THAT YOU WILL WELL AND FAITHFULLY DISCHARGE THE DUTIES OF THE OFFICE ON WHICH YOU ARE ABOUT TO ENTER: SO HELP YOU GOD?**

With this being the oath, I challenge our officials to step up and execute their commitment to this oath and enact legislation that will allow for a national referendum on a constitutional amendment for a balanced budget. I say this because this oath, swears them to "defend the Constitution of the United States against all enemies, foreign and domestic." And. in this case, the budget deficit is the threat to our Constitution. They are the only ones that can save the country from this domestic threat.

We have a thing called the debt ceiling, this being a top dollar amount we can spend over our actual income. Once it is set at a level, it never comes down but in order to raise the ceiling, Congress must take the time to vote to do this. When this comes about, there is always a war on spending cut threats in both the House and the Senate. If we had a balanced budget amendment, there would be no need for a debt ceiling. Therefore, no time would be used consuming a spending cut war, this in itself would save money and a lot of stress. Furthermore, we currently have mandatory cuts (Budget Cuts – Sequestration) that go into effect when our budget does get to high. Our current "checks and balances" on this issue call for federal employees that have nothing to do with how the money is spent to be sacrificed.

I think our priorities are a little out of focus.

Here's a thought. What if when the budget goes into deficit, otherwise not balanced, the first cuts are the very employees that allowed it to happen. This means, The President, and ALL of Congress as well. I list these because; the President is responsible for proposing the budget, and signing off on it. Besides, he is the Commander In Chief, he must lead by example. Therefore, ultimately he is responsible. I site all of Congress, because they are the ones that ultimately put the budget together, they decide just what is going to be in it, and they do the final voting on the budget. They decide not only if there will be a deficit, but how much of one.

Moreover, if we are going to use this automatic budget cut system the protection process needs to stipulate that there is to be no "retroactive" paychecks for this action. This again makes no sense to me, if we have to stop the money flow because we are too broke, then how after we agree that we can spend money again do we have enough money to give all the money we saved last week away again? This one will never make sense to me.

I believe there is a simple solution.

This is something that needs to be added to the "Bill of Rights" WE have the right to.... a balanced budget. It needs to be added so we will always have the right to "have a chance at a future equal to that of our forefathers". In the Declaration of Independence (The greatest document ever written – my opinion) it states;

"...*Life, Liberty and the pursuit of Happiness...*" As well, in the Preamble of our Constitution it states "...*insure* **domestic Tranquility**....*promote the general* **Welfare***, and secure the Blessings of Liberty to ourselves and our* **Posterity***...*" And finally I simply site - *President Washington's Farwell address.*

It does not take a brain surgeon, or even a smart economist, to tell you none of the aforementioned cornerstones can be obtained/fulfilled with/by a government that runs its budgets in the negative numbers, especially the size of negative numbers we are working with.

In a nut shell; my thoughts are, there needs to be either a balanced budget amendment **OR** a "checks and balances" system that holds the very people that cause the problem, responsible for the fix.

This is as good a spot as any for a side thought on a political topic of targeting votes;

I get a kick out of the grumbling argument that there are black people that only voted for President Obama because he was black. Oh my goodness, that sounds horrifically racist. But I ask, is that any worse than the number of whites that did not vote for him because he was black? I further ask, why was it okay for John McCain to have a woman on his ticket with the goal of getting the women to vote for him because of her? Why is it a given that any presidential candidate will win his/her home state? (Would this be the time to point out even Walter Mondale 1984) People have always done this and always will. Whether it is race, gender, religion or some other common bond, people tend to want to see someone that they can relate to in one way or another win. It's a simple emotional boost; if their person wins, in a sense, they win too.

Oh wow, all I can say is, can we find something, anything, better to think about or talk about on the nightly news shows than speculation as to how or why someone else may or may not have voted. Oh Boy.

My bigger concern is for those that simply vote for the incumbent.

Chapter 7

My Thoughts on War

My cliff notes version of this chapter is short and simple – participate in war only as a last resort. My movie quote answer is from "War Games" 1983 –

"A strange game, the only winning move is not to play, how about a nice game of chess?"

My historical answer – read President George Washington's Farewell Address.

However, my long answer is, war has been a part of human behavior going back as far has history has record. Our country, as all others, came into existence by way of war. As well, in our 238+ years, we have had a few additional wars to say the least. Some wars had a clear cut purpose while others have been very controversial. In every case, there has always been at least one person that was opposed to our participation in that war. Moreover, in every war, there has always been and will always be at least one person that had nothing to do with the cause or the solution of the war that will be killed because of the war, so I will always say, war should always be the last resort.

My biggest question for this topic about war and America's involvement will be, how does it come to be? What justifies war? Since the closest thing to a written definition for the purpose of/for war is the words that are in the oath of office for the federal elected officials, *"to protect against...foreign and domestic."* Therefore, we as citizens can rest assured that the reasons for going to war will always be changing. It is clear that the justification(s) of war or for going into war will always depend on the views and/or values of the elected officials at any given time. It will be based on what they feel is a threat to our country at any given time. This is why I have been so befuddled over the words and actions of our congress' over the last 15 plus years, and their dealings with the wars in Iraq and Afghanistan here in the 21st century. These were congress' that clearly showed through budget deficits after budget deficits that they allowed to accumulate, that they clearly had (have) no true desire to do what is in the best interest of this country in the long term. Yet, they were willing to call for a war against other countries.

I find it a touch hypocritical for a congress that has been allowing a budget deficit of trillions of dollars to tell us they think or believe a group or groups of people from another country are more of a threat to our future than they are. Furthermore, I will go back to the previously sited document by President Washington. In this Farewell Address, he deeply covers the warnings of going to war. He clearly states war should always be of a last resort. And, at all cost, stay out of any other country's wars. While the issues that are going on in the lands on the other side of the pond may seem like a clear and "present" danger, our budget issues are by far a much greater threat to our existence.

Humanization of War

Over the years, war has always created devastating collateral damage, and as humanity has progressed, we have attempted to clean war up so as to eliminate the collateral damage. Therefore, we put rules in place as to how and what the opposing military's can do during war time.

My thought on that plan; let's see, we have a group(s) of people that are not happy with the way things are going, so they decide to change things through the use of deadly violence (Hum). Do we expect these people to care if they are going by the rules that someone else set forth? Furthermore, the people(s) that set these rules lived decades ago in lands far far away, and we are really still thinking these rules are going to matter. Oh boy!!!

The Geneva Convention;

War and The Geneva Convention; there was a time when a saying such as "all's fair in love and war" was accurate. Then the media got involved. Now, well now even war has to play to a Hollywood script of some sort so the media will approve, while love still has no rules. The Geneva Conventions created or developed a tone for the purpose of civilizing war; it had a goal to make sure innocent/noncombatants were protected form a war they were not involved in. However, as time has passed, the only countries that are expected to abide by this Geneva Convention are the U.S., Great Britain, France and Israel.

Here are a couple of examples. Our media covers as much front line action as they can. In the process of this coverage, we end up seeing more of the war in our living room than we should. We know from factual media coverage as well as our wounded returning men and women that improvised explosive devices (ied's) are being used. These devices are being used by the opposing forces to either kill or mime our military personnel. By rule of The

Geneva Convention is allowed. However, the problem with the use of these devices is, they kill at random. I agree that the goal is to kill our troops, but by using these devices like they do, inevitably, non-combative people end up being killed.

I have to use the "politically correct" words of "non-combative people" because I cannot in good faith use the words "innocent people." I can't use the word innocent here, because to me, all the men and women that fight for our country are innocent. None of these soldiers had anything to do with the start, continuation or closure of any of the wars. Thus, I cannot use the word "innocent" when referring to just non fighting people that are killed in war.

Thus, when people that are not soldiers are killed, it is now a violation of the Geneva Convention, and these "IED's" are a clear violation. Yet there are no "referees" out on the war field to call fouls. So again, I state the only ones that are expected to go by the rules are the U.S., Great Britain, France and Israel.

Furthermore, the use of suicide bombers as a weapon is way beyond anything any person could ever justify. To me, there is no way this makes any sense. Here you are trying to change the way things are because you're not happy with the way life is for you, and what do you do? You go and kill yourself and take other people with you, people that had absolutely nothing to do with you and your "bad hair day." That is so stupid. Now even if you do win, you still lose because you are no longer here to enjoy the changed way of life you so desperately wanted. Now that has to be the worst idea ever.

My thoughts on this; this may sound cold but, let war be war. As stated, war has been around as long as man. Certain things are always clear about war; it is not fun, it is not clean and it always destroys lives. To attempt to humanize war or even cut down on the collateral damage of war is twisted thinking. Here is why I say that. I understand that it is wrong for a person that just so happens to be living in a war zone to be killed. Yes that is a horrific tragedy. However, is that tragedy any worse than that of the parents/families of any of the soldiers that are killed in/during these wars? These parents and families also have to deal with a lifetime of grief over the death of their son or daughter. Therefore, if all people know that the rules of war are to win at any and all cost and that all sides are playing by the same rules (none), our present "War on Terrorism" would not have lasted this long! Common sense tells us that when we have to do war by "The Rules" while our opponents get to write their own rules, we are setting ourselves up for bad days.

There was a time when the leader of a country was also the leader when that country marched into war. To me, this only makes sense, since the war is all about the leader(s) having different points of view to start with. Here is an idea. Instead of taking the young innocent youth and telling them to go fight a complete stranger over a dispute that neither of them had anything to do with, let the rules be, that we send our fearless leaders to fight each other. The same leaders that are willing to wage the war should be the ones to fight the war(s).

We are all wrapped up in what is going on in other countries and so fearful that their issues MIGHT come here next. My thoughts are that we are living in a media age that lets us be up to the minute in real time on issues all over the world. Forty years ago, the issues we are waging war over would not even be of interest. The issues in the Middle East are nothing new; this type of action has been going on since before the "holy" books were written. The difference is we now all have cell phones and internet to make us think we are right in the mix.

My thoughts on all of this can be best explained with a look at our "net gain" in our present wars in the Middle East, that being the War on Terror dating from 9/11/ 2001. We were given a surprise sneak attack that killed 2,740 people in or around the World Trade Centers and in planes. As well, an additional 236 rescue workers, for a total of 2976 people died as a direct result of this sneaky blindsided attack. This does not take into consideration the devastation it has caused in the lives of those surviving family members. Our response was to make the attackers pay by us going to war with them. To date, the death toll of American men and women alone in "Operation Enduring Freedom" is: 6811. We have lost more lives in the payback phase than we did in the attack. However, let's add this number to the lives lost in the 9/11 attack and our total body count is 9,787(+) men and women that have died in this war. I can do nothing but shake my head. There was a professional football player that gave up his million-dollar career to give his life for this cause. How many of our elected officials can say the same? They waged the war but would not go fight it.

My proposed solution;

Scrap the Geneva Conventions and let war be war. I don't have a problem with rules, as long as they are in an arena that can be monitored, and war is no such arena. Picture this; the people decide to do a sneak attack on us. They take down the World Trade Centers and we lose 2976(+) lives, people from all walks of life. People died that had no clue what was going on. Now here is our response. We look into the event and find out the root violators. Then bomb the heck out of them and theirs. Yes, on the surface that sounds harsh and cold, but is it? To date, we have lost nearly 10,000 lives and spent trillions of dollars and what have we accomplished? Not a thing. If anything, we have gone backwards. Now, we are now looked upon as a much weaker nation than we were before. This is not President Obama's doing. If we would have taken the page from President G.H.W. Bush (41) and used our superior technology, we would have accomplished two things. One fewer lives would have been lost and two, we would have sent yet another message that you cannot hide from us. We can and we will get you from anywhere and we will not lose any sleep over it.

Rebuttal-

- This type of military attack would cause other countries not to like us. My response - Yeah, like the attack on 9/11 was a sign of love.
- This type of military action would cause more attacks on us. My response - I say that is wrong, but let's find out. As it is, we have lost more actual lives in the ground war than we did in the actual attack, which means we have also had more families destroyed as collateral damage.

I am one of the lucky parents; my son came home. However, I can feel for the families that had losses. It only makes it worse knowing that we still have the technology that was used in the Gulf War of 1990-91. In this war, there were a total of 294 lives lost, but the relentless air bombardment set the stage for a quick ending of this war. We left Iraq with a message to all the other nations. That message was a strong one of- **you mess with us, and you feel the wrath.**

I close with this thought;

The best offense is a strong defense, but just because we are the strongest does not mean we have to prove it every day. War should be a last resort, not a way of life.

I have noticed that WWII was the last time our country came together as a whole to strive for a victory. In every war we have been in since the WWII, it is as if war is a side event and our country just keeps on going as if nothing is or has happened. We all still go to work or school. We all still have all our social events. What gets to me the most is that we all still go on with all our holiday practices. I understand the argument that we are a free country and we cannot change our ways of life because of some terrorist in another country. That sounds like a good answer, but it is not a healthy one. The truth is, we have changed our lives, and we continue to change every time we send a soldier off to war. I am saying that we are getting to the point that war is always somewhere else, war is only on the news, and war is too easy. I would like to see a slight change; I would like to see it established that when we as a country go to war, we all understand that there is in fact a war. I am all for curtailing some, if not most, of our holiday events and celebrations. I would like to see a measure before congress that says in times of war, that elected government officials get a large reduction in pay as a gesture of helping to pay for the war, and that no elected government official gets vacation time.

These are just a couple of my thoughts on how we could bring our country together. All of us could be showing the men and women that are sacrificing everything for us that we are willing to sacrifice a little for them. After this chapter I would say, if this were my event, I would say it is time to say the pledge of allegiance again. Oh yes you are right, this is my event. Well let's get on with it;

"I pledge allegiance to the flag of the United States of America, and to the republic for which it stands, the greatest nation of them all, indivisible, with liberty and justice for all."

Damn, I love this country!

Chapter 8

Immigration

Here we are proclaiming ourselves as a free nation, a nation that was once proud to accept and display the Statue of Liberty that carries this Inscription.

Give me your tired, your poor,
Your huddled masses, yearning to breath free,
The wretched refuse of your teeming shore,
Send these, the homeless, tempest tost to me,
I lift my lamp beside the golden door.

Author: Emma Lazarus

We boast that we are the greatest nation on earth, while at the same time, we are building a wall to keep people out. We are acting as if the immigration issue is something new, yet our 26th president, Teddy Roosevelt, spent many years addressing this very issue a hundred years ago.

Theodore Roosevelt's ideas on immigrants and being an AMERICAN in 1907.

"In the first place, we should insist that if the immigrant who comes here in good faith becomes an American and assimilates himself to us, he shall be treated on an exact equality with everyone else, for it is an outrage to discriminate against any such man because of creed, or birthplace, or origin. But this is predicated upon the person's becoming in every facet an American and nothing but an American...There can be no divided allegiance here. Any man who says he is an American, but something else also, isn't an American at all. We have room for but one flag, the American flag... We have room for but one language here, and that is the English language... and we have room for but one sole loyalty and that is a loyalty to the American people."

Theodore Roosevelt 1907

This was not only an issue for him during his time in office but it continued right up to the day that he died.

The following is an expert from a letter he wrote on January 3, 1919 to the president of the American Defense Society. It was read publicly at a meeting on January 5, 1919. Roosevelt died the next day, on January 6, 1919.

The actual text from Teddy Roosevelt's letter is below. There are a few minor differences from the original such as changing "man" to "person" but the content is virtually identical.

This was our 26th President pointing out a hundred years ago that we had immigration issues. Now, if I may add something that to most (older) people today will carry more historical importance on this issue. In 1985 Cheech & Chong released their album "Get Out Of My Room" which featured the single "Born In East L.A." Furthermore, the song "Low Rider" *by War in 1975* was the opening theme song for the Cheech and Chong movie "Up In Smoke" *(1978)*. This shows that not only was there an immigration issue at that time, but that it had been around long enough that people were finding ways to make money off the issue. (*Though the song was originally about motorcycles, the movie brought it to be the term for low riding cars with hydraulic systems made popular my Hispanic immigrants.*) This is a major indicator that immigration was an issue at least 30 plus years prior to our current dilemma.

Here we are in 2015 and we are all up in arms about out of control immigration. Everyone is pointing fingers at the Federal government for letting this happen, as well as demanding that our government find a way to stop it, and I mean stop it, in its tracks. It has gotten to the point that we are willing to build a wall to surround our country and have armed guards walking the wall/boarder as a way to address this issue. I find this wall idea to be so backward, so anti-American, and downright hypocritical. In the northeast gateway to our America, we have the open arms of the Statue of Liberty, while in the southwest we want to build the "Great Wall of "Feardom."

In our world history, there have been two other countries with border walls, China and Germany. With this I have to ask, do we seriously want future history books to have our country listed alongside of these? Furthermore, if my memory serves correct, it was one of our most renowned, and respected presidents that on June 12, 1987 gave the following speech;

We welcome change and openness; for we believe that freedom and security go together, that the advance of human liberty can only strengthen the cause of world peace. There is

one sign the Soviets can make that would be unmistakable, that would advance dramatically the cause of freedom and peace. General Secretary Gorbachev, if you seek peace, if you seek prosperity for the Soviet Union and Eastern Europe, if you seek liberalization, come here to this gate. Mr. Gorbachev, open this gate. Mr. Gorbachev, tear down this wall! *(Ronald Reagan Presidential Library).*

Here on the immigration issue, I find it so amazing that our private sector is looking for the government to be the one(s) to stop this problem. Here I see that the people in our private sector of America do not want to take responsibility for their own actions and accept that our present illegal immigration problem is a direct result of the practices that the private sector, the business sector as well as the humanitarian equal rights groups have created.

This is correct, and my thoughts are that we cannot hold our government responsible for this mess, nor can we look for them to be the sole solution. If we want a true and long-term solution to our illegal immigration issues, it will have to be the private sector and business sector that take the point in fixing this issue. The solution is not hard nor is it expensive. It really is quite simple. We need to stop pandering/catering to the illegals. We are all but begging for the illegals to come to the U.S. from most of the Latin American countries. We have everything set up to speak their language. We sell their food, we provide them with food and healthcare, and worst of all, it is a violation of "THEIR" civil rights if they get asked for an identification and or documentation papers by any law enforcement. Let me re-present the speech given 100 years ago by President Teddy Roosevelt, I will highlight and bold print the points that he made way back then that are most prevalent with the issue today.

*We should insist that if **the immigrant who comes here does in good faith become an American and assimilates himself to us** he shall be treated on an exact equality with everyone else, for it is an outrage to discriminate against any such man because of creed or birth-place or origin.*

But this is predicated upon the man's becoming

in every fact an American and nothing but an American. If he tries to keep segregated with men of his own origin and separated from the rest of America, then he isn't doing his part as an American. There can be no divided allegiance here. . . We have room for but one language here, and that is the English language, for we intend to see that the crucible turns our people out as Americans, **of American nationality, and not as dwellers in a polyglot boarding-house; and we have room for but one soul loyalty, and that is loyalty to the American people.**

If we take the time to re-read this letter written by President Teddy Roosevelt, we would see that it is not our government that is to blame, but our private sector. Our push for equal rights has taken on a life of its own. We have gone from a country bound by segregation and discrimination to a country of no root identity. We, as a country, were forced by laws to open the can of equality, and now we are overdosing in it. For over 150 years, we were a blindly divided nation prior to the civil rights movements of the 1950's and 1960's. It took the U. S. Supreme Court rulings to open our eyes to our discriminative ways. In less than 60 years, we have decided that equal rights mean we have to pander to each and every person that shows up and is or has a "difference" in some way. On the surface, going the extra mile to make sure we are creating "equality" sounds good, but it really is not. We have stepped right over the very issue that the civil rights were enacted for and moved on to others, which in turn has created our illegal immigration issue.

My point here is the language barrier. Meaning that now as a country we have lost our identity. We have an official language of English, and yet, everywhere you go, Spanish is readily available. This is where we are going wrong. It is not our government's fault. Our own business sector and private sector that is making it so welcoming for the immigrants to come here and dwell without any problems. President Roosevelt was clear then, and it shows now that he was right. Immigration is fine, as long as we maintain that we are one America, and we have one language, which is English. However, our civil rights activists are so worried that we will hurt someone's feelings and therefore violating their equal rights that we are pushing for Spanish in our schools and even being pushed as being an official second language. Moreover, our business world has gotten so greedy for the dollar that they have adopted the ease of the "Española" option on every electronic device. No matter who you call anymore, you get a prompt to press one for English or dos para Española. Almost every store has cash out lines that convert to Spanish.

To me, there is a simple solution; if you want to live in the U.S., you have to speak English. I know when my wife and I travel to Mexico; they don't speak English for us. So why are we in the U.S. making Spanish so readily available? Here is a real apples to apples comparison; as I have said, my wife and I live in Louisville Kentucky, about a mile from a Wal-Mart store that has all the Spanish conversion conveniences a person could ask for. On the other hand in December of 2015 we were in Port of Vallarta Mexico on one of our cruise ship ports of call, and there was a Wal-Mart not 200 yards from the port. We walked over to visit and compare; what we found was, only one person spoke English and none of the cash registers were equipped to convert to English, we had to have assistance to convert. Here I will say, I do not expect the people or businesses in Mexico to accommodate visitors for not speaking Spanish. I believe it is my responsibility to have a grasp of their language before I go, rather than them knowing mine. However, in the USA we are doing it different, this is why I say our illegal immigration problem is not solely our government's fault. Rather it is the fault of all our businesses converting to Spanish and making it so easy to come here and live. I am willing to bet that there is not a court in our land that would be willing to take a case of civil rights violations based on the grounds that they were not provided a Spanish language option at the grocery store or in a restaurant. Our equal rights laws' say we have to respect people that are deaf or are hearing impaired. There is no way the courts could tie that into having to provide for a person that does not speak English (exception for people arrested and needing translators for the courtroom, but then again, if they knew English when they got here, they might not have ended up in jail).

I know it is all nice to want to be able to speak the language in the case of an emergency, but we are making it so easy that when the people in Mexico have an emergency, they come here, and then they never go home. This problem is so bad that I was in a supermarket in Louisville, Kentucky and I asked a lady a question, and her response was, "I don't speak English." My response was, "What? How in the world does a person get all the way to Louisville Kentucky and not speak English?" Now, granted she could be traveling, but I don't see Louisville as a hot spot for Mexican tourists!

What we are doing is making it easy for the illegal immigrants to come over and then blend in without ever being detected. We have made it easy to avoid detection by basically creating an underground Spanish society for all the illegals to live and thrive in. With our private and business communities catering to the Spanish language, the immigrants have no reason to assimilate. To make matters worse, we now even have our presidential candidates catering to the Spanish population by speaking Spanish themselves.

I have a hard time thinking that one President 100 years ago was so emphatic about our country being a United States and welcoming all immigrants but requiring that they assimilate. We only have room for one language and that language is English. Now, 100 years later, we have people running for president and giving speeches in Spanish, this nothing less than a way of openly endorsing a dual America. This is patriotic digression.

Another incident I noticed that I will never understand nor accept an explanation if one is given was the boxing match on May 2, 2015 between **Floyd Mayweather, Jr. vs. Manny Pacquiao.** Mayweather was born in Michigan and fights out of

California, while Pacquiao is from the Philippines. The fight was in Las Vegas, Nevada, which last I knew was in the United States. I sat comfortably waiting as the fight was about to begin and then they announced it was time for the main event. They started this main event just like they started all main sporting events I have ever witnessed, by signing the National Anthem. I was talking to my friend when we realized they were singing the Mexican National Anthem first, then the Philippines National Anthem, and lastly the United States National Anthem. To this day, I have no idea why the Mexican National Anthem was played, neither fighter was from Mexico and the fight was in the United States. There is no acceptable explanation that can justify this.

I think our priorities are a little out of focus.

President Roosevelt was not only clear on his points, but he was correct; we have but one America, one language, one flag and one nation. We have made it so easy for illegals to live here that there is no deterrent to keep them from coming and once they are here there is no reason for them to have to leave. We have made it so easy for them to blend in that there is no reason for them to assimilate. Bottom line is that this does not fall squarely on our government, and our private and business sectors have to step up and make some hard changes.

However, I will say the government does have a little responsibility of their own on this issue. I see one particular thing that I think the government could have done that would have helped cut down on or even prevented a lot of our immigration issues.

Here is my view on how the government could help things. I have mentioned this plan to a few of my friends that I have always thought to be smarter than me, and they all said it could not work but would not or could not give me a reason as to why. So that makes me like my plan that much more.

Here it is; way back in the 1970's our politicians started working in this thing called NAFTA (North American Free Trade Act). Well it was kicked around for a couple of decades until it was finally signed into law as of January 1, 1994. Here is my thing. If this deal would have had the language that stated that any U.S. company that took its factories to another country and then brought the products back to the U.S. for sale, than they would be mandated to have to pay the workers in those factories U.S. prevailing wages or have your products hit with very high tariffs on their return.

To me this would provide a double line of protection. First, it would cause any and all companies to have to think it over real hard as to whether they really want or need to move their manufacturing out of the U.S. Next, if they still chose to move the factories and paid the higher labor wages, the standard of living in countries such as Mexico, would improve to a level that gives people a reason to stay in their homeland.

So if we in the U.S. stop pandering to the Spanish language or if our companies that build factories in Mexico were to pay the Mexican workers more money, the immigration problem would be reduced.

I do have a side thought I would like to put in right here in the immigration chapter. On the issue of immigration, one of the complications is the language barrier. I do have a proposed solution for the language barrier problem. My solution does not come about because of my inability to speak Spanish. My solution comes from a situation with my oldest granddaughter, and after thinking about it, I think it would be a solution to all language barriers worldwide.

When my granddaughter was young, she had an undiagnosed internal ear issue. While she was fully capable of hearing and understanding people, this issue was preventing her from being able to form words, and therefore she could not speak herself. So, it was looking like we were all going to have to learn sign language. It was at this time that I thought, hum why don't we already know it? I got to thinking, what if sign language was taught to all students worldwide starting in Kindergarten and lasting through twelfth grade?

Therefore, I propose that each country not only have their native language but also teach sign language in all of the schools. This would allow for all countries to have their own distinct language, that gives each of us a sense of a unique identity, but also have symbol sign language that is universal. This way, whenever anyone travels anywhere in the world for whatever reason, they will still be able to communicate.

As for our illegal immigration problem, our private sector needs to step up and take some responsibility. The largest part of the fix here is on them. Stop the phone options for Spanish, stop the translators in our places of business, stop the Spanish wording on products in stores, and by all means, STOP the social program benefits from going to anyone that cannot speak English fluently.

Chapter 9

Gun Control

Our second amendment has been a point of argument for as long as I can remember. Again, this is another argument that makes no sense to me. Our politicians are allowing these issues to become polarizing ones. By them not getting together, talking, and working out solutions, it allows the news media talk shows to sell a polarizing spin to the public. They are allowing for the debate to build into an all or nothing scenario. People are asking for gun control that can make a difference, not gun control that would eliminate guns.

I personally have no use for guns; I don't like them and feel that they are being touted as being both the cure and the cause for our murder rate problem. I hear people argue that they need them for defense, yet in all cases, a gun is an offensive weapon. I know that just got a whole lot of people to throw the book and curse me. But let me explain!

By all practical definitions, offense is a first strike practice while defense is a reaction that is used to detour or stop an offensive action.

- I am carrying my gun for defensive reasons and a person steps in front of me, gun in their hand pointed right at me and says, "you are about to die." What are the chances of me defending myself with my gun? The answer for all you that are still thinking – ZERO!

- If you have a gun to go hunting, from whom are you defending yourself????

- The only time a gun can be presented in a defensive manner is when an intruder invades your home with you in it.

So, I cannot accept the argument that guns are needed for defense.

However, I am still a big believer in the second amendment. I still believe that people should have the right to keep and bear arms. Though, we must keep in mind that with every "Right" or "Freedom" we have comes conditions and responsibilities. The first amendment gives us the right to free speech, but that does not mean we can or should say whatever we want when or wherever we want. There is something about freedom and rights that not all people understand. That is, people have to be taught how to understand and use the freedoms and rights we have.

Furthermore, I hear people using the argument that "Those rights were given to us so nobody can take them away." Sorry, by that is far from the truth. None of our rights were given to us; all of them were fought for and they were earned. People died so that we could have these rights. So for anyone to think that the second amendment saying that we have the right to bear arms means each and every person can simply go pick one up at your corner store, no questions asked, is gravely mistaken. Like I said, these rights were earned; they were fought for and earned 238+ years ago. Today, we all need to respect them and earn the right to exercise and benefit from them.

It is bewildering to me that the big money powerful people of the NRA that fight with deep pockets and tireless passion for an open, broad and liberal meaning of the second amendment are quiet as church mice when it comes to the meaning of the fifth amendment. I mean most of the people that need the Fifth Amendment do so because of the guns they had the right to carry. This makes me wonder, just whose side the NRA is really on? For me, I do not have a problem with responsible people having guns. I am, however, a big fan of doing deep thorough background checks to make sure the people we deem to be responsible really are.

My belief is that guns are not the problem; the problems are with the hands that the guns are in. This is equal to the argument that if a person drives a car into another person or people the car is not the problem. The problem is with the person driving the car. If we add alcohol to the mix, we still do not blame that car; so, why do we hold a gun to a different standard?

I would like to propose one idea for this issue. Like I said, I am all for the extensive in-depth background check but if we are honest about this issue, the vast majority of gun crimes are not committed by people that will have background check issues, or background checks done at all. Gun control only comes up when there is a big noticeable tragic event that kills an important person or multiple people in a media attractive way. The vast majority of gun crimes are committed by unnoticed people on the streets. Every year, more people are killed in single "murder as a thing to do" type of crime than all mass shootings combined. Touching on an earlier point, we need to make sure that people that have guns are responsible and accountable people, (I have another book coming on this very subject) but until we have that, I think we might be able to try something else.

I am not a big gun expert but I am thinking about ways to give the police an edge on catching the criminal faster when they do leave a bullet behind. Here is my thinking; I know that every time a gun is sold, the serial number has to be logged and registered. Then, if the police recover a gun, they can trace the gun back to the purchaser. Well, what if we had a way to track the bullet back to the gun and the purchaser? Here I mean, every gun has a different barrel rifling. This is how the police match a bullet from a scene to a specific gun once they get the gun. Well, I propose that every gun that is produced be fired and record the rifling. That record is logged into the computer with the serial number. Now, when the police recover a bullet from a crime, they can take the rifling's from the recovered bullet, put them into the computer, much like they do with fingerprints, and see what gun the bullet came from and who owns it. This would give the police a new and faster way to start an investigation when a gun is used.

I already hear the counter argument; there are already too many guns on the street being used in crimes now, so starting this type of system would not help. My response to that is that it is partly true and partly false. The important part is false. You have to start some place, and one day the guns being sold today will be the guns used in crimes. And if in all of time, one case is solved from this process, it will be worth it, at least to the victim's family if not anybody else.

Chapter 10

Climate Change

The issue of climate change is a prime example of my claim that people in groups or organizations with pre-set platforms lose the ability to be open minded. First, I cannot believe there is even a debate over this. Furthermore, I am flabbergasted at the extreme points that people are voicing.

1. I have heard some people that are sold on the climate change theory say that the sea level will rise so high in the next 70 years that New York City will be completely under water.
   a. I personally think that is a bit extreme. The bad part about this extremism is that it becomes counterproductive. People hear this as "Chicken Little," and give little too no credence to the whole theory.
2. That the planet is so big and has been around for so long how could anyone believe that the actions of humans could possibly have that big of a negative effect on the climate, specially over the last 200 years.

a. This logic for denial actually is the best logic I have heard to endorse the theory.

b. Less than two hundred ago, the Great Lakes water system was clean, healthy and producing life as well as supporting life. However, by the 1960's and 1970's the Great Lakes were dying, Lake Eire in fact was pronounced dead at that time. After studies and testes it was determined that it was the acts and behaviors of humans that caused the Great Lakes to get that way. It was the very pollutants from humans that were killing the lakes eco-system.

c. Then, there is the phenomenon of "Acid Rain" that was first detected in the 1850's, just after the advent of the industrial revolution that has been directly tied to human activities and behaviors.

d. Because of human behaviors over the last 100 years, the fish worldwide are tainted with poisons and toxins to the point that eating fish more than twice a week is harmful to our health, yes I can see where the argument that people could not have an impact on our climate holds water. (Pardon the pun)

Two-thirds of the planet is covered with water, one of the essential elements needed for life. Now, it is clear that we as humans through our drive and belief of being "superior" have not just made a negative effect on the water system; we have made a HUGE negative effect on it. So if we have undeniably been able to make such a negative effect on the water system, why would a person not accept that we could be have the same type of negative effect on the whole planetary eco-system? If a person wants to argue that there is a difference between the water system and the atmosphere, I think one of us needs to go back to school. I will concede there is a difference; however, one cannot live without the other.

It has been determined that the manmade fertilizer used by humans to improve plant growth was the major cause (but not only cause) of the water pollution. It has also been determined that the high levels of methane being produced by the increased needs of humans are causing harmful effects on our atmosphere. The argument on this is that methane is produced naturally so why is it such a big deal that humans are producing it too. This is almost a good argument except methane has a negative effect on the atmosphere whether it is produced naturally or by humans. Since nature is going to do what nature does, we have to be responsible for what we can control. Willfully adding more negative gas to what is naturally produced is just irresponsible. Also, using the argument that there is already methane gas being made naturally so why should it matter if we make more is the equivalent to saying people are going to get sick and die so why should it matter if people use crack cocaine. The answer, because it is wrong.

On this issue, the question is not whether the science is right or wrong on climate change, but rather are we right or wrong on thinking it matters. This whole argument on whether we as humans are causing irreparable harm to the atmosphere and thus going to cause the end of life is ridiculous. In my world, there is a taught practice that we are responsible for fixing the broken world, or otherwise said; we are responsible for leaving this world in a better way then we received it. This is not a farfetched ideal; we all teach our children to pick up their toys when they are done with them. We teach them to clean their room, clean the house, as well as the yard. We teach our children the very practice of "leaving things in a better way than when they started" but yet, as adults, we do not want to hold ourselves to the same practice.

Here is a question – What is the Greater threat to our planet -- asteroid or man? -- In either case, we are doomed. The chances of us/man being able to move an asteroid off its course is slim, but the chances of us/man coming together to agree on whether we/man is the cause of global warming is impossible, let alone agreeing on a plan on how to prevent/fix it. Let's look at just a couple of points to ponder.

1. What gets hotter and holds heat longer, concrete or dirt? Yes you are right, concrete, and we as humans are producing more and more concrete and asphalt every day.
   a. Let's think about the winter weather for a minute. In the winter when the temperatures are below freezing but the sun is out, why does the snow and ice melt on the concrete and asphalt areas but not on the grassy areas? Hum
   b. And all this heat is radiating into the atmosphere.
2. What gets hotter and holds heat longer, concrete or wood? Again you are right, it is concrete. And we as humans are producing more and more concrete every day.
3. Look at what happens to the inside temperature of a car in the summer time. We still don't want

to believe humans can or are making an impact on the environment.

There is absolutely nothing wrong with being better stewards of this planet while we are alive. We argue that the Federal government is wrong and irresponsible by having this financial deficit. It is said that we are wrong for leaving all this debt for our children and grandchildren to have to pay. Yet, we don't have the same mindset about the eco-system.   There is nothing wrong with doing something just because it is the right thing to do. Whether we are hurting the environment or not is not the issue, the issue is; is it is the right thing to do. You keep your room clean, you keep your house clean, and you keep your yard clean as well you help to keep your neighborhood clean, why? Because it is the right thing to do. If we do our part to stop being so dirty, the world will take care of the rest. This should not be a political issue, this is an ethical issue.

Chapter 11

Abortion

Here are my thoughts on abortion. While this is a very controversial issue, it really does not have to be. While I am personally opposed to abortion, that is not the point. I cannot get pregnant. Granted, there is the argument that while I can't get pregnant, I am still involved in the issue because I am capable of creating a pregnancy. While I will agree with the point in principle, I still maintain that it is not a valid point in the argument as a whole. The only validity that point would have, would be on my having any say so in the case of the pregnancy I am personally involved in; it does not give me any say so in any other pregnancy.

One of my points of reason is that I am a firm believer in individual choice. I just think that if I don't want someone else telling me what to do on my issues, who am I to try to tell someone else what to do on their issues. This is one of those things in life that I have to accept. I may not like it, but it is what it is. And by opening the door to banning a woman's right to choice on abortion, no matter what the reason, we are in all actuality closing the door on our "Constitutional Bill of Rights. Because once precedence is established for stopping the rights of "another" person it will make it that much easier to start stripping away all of our rights one by one.

Furthermore, I see a difference in the two sides of this argument. The pro-choice argument is based on an individual having the privacy to make a personal choice in their life. While the pro-life argument is to allow "Other people" to call the shots on what other people can do in or with their lives. Nobody in the pro-choice group is calling for or demanding for abortion to mandatory, or for a person to be forced to have an abortion if they don't want to. No insurance company that provides coverage is making it mandatory for anyone to have an abortion. What if the argument was going the other way, what if we had a mandatory abortion law as is in China? Would we all not be arguing that the abortion laws were an infringement on our rights? Yes we would, so here the argument is just the same, just from the other side of view.

I do understand that this abortion issue is not solely about a lady's right to have a personal choice when it comes to her body. I understand that a big portion of this abortion issue has to do with somebody with a religious soul trying to save another person's wayward sole. I know that sounded very harsh, but I could find no way to candy coat it. Now, we are into the religious realm of this issue. When it comes to the religious points of view, as a Jewish person, I do enjoy a good argument. To site a couple of cases in Biblical history, Jews do have a record of arguing with God himself, and actually winning on a couple of occasions.

1. Abraham argued with God when God was set to destroy Sodom and Gomorrah. God set the number of good people to find at one hundred, and Abraham argued with him until he got God all the way down to ten. (I have often wondered if this is where the first record of the term "Jewed someone down" occurred. I know that to some people that can be an offensive phrase but I mean no harm. I simply look at that and say, well it fits, and go on with a smile.)
2. There is the Jacob confrontation, when he spends the night fighting with the angel. He does so well that in the morning, the angel tells Jacob that from that point on he will be known as Israel.
3. And there is no way I can pass up Moses and his arguments with God on a couple of occasions while he was on the mountain, He won some and he lost some.

With that stated, I will acknowledge I am no Abraham, Jacob or Moses but the point remains. It is okay to argue a religious point as long as it is a good argument, even if you argue with God. So when my points seem to be contrary to what is an acceptable "religious" norm, I am not being disrespectful nor anti-religious. I am simply making a counter point to the ones that have already been brought to the table. Just because a person brings God into the situation does not automatically make them right.

It seems that the arguments for preventing or outlawing abortion are rooted in religion or the belief that God is the creator of life, and therefore abortion is murder. I have heard that all pregnancies are an act of God or a miracle that God chose to happen. Well that sounds good on the surface. However, if that is the argument at hand I have to ask, what does it mean when a pregnant lady has a miscarriage? I have heard it said that a miscarriage is okay because that is God's will and that it is/was all part of God's plan. Well how do we know that? If so, why is it okay for God to have a plan to kill the baby? I know this is where a few people (most) will start to have issues with my thoughts. But, here is where I ask that you take some time to think about this. I hear people say on regular basis that "if it's

156

God's will" and "if God wants it to happen it will."
My wife and I have heated debates over this a lot.

The "God's plan" thing just does not work for
me; it is used in an insulting way. The other day,
here in Kentucky, there was a terrible tragedy on the
highway. One of the rescue workers was hit and
killed by a passing car on. The worker's uncle, who
was also a rescue worked, and a deeply religious
man explained to the news that the accident was
okay because it was all meant to be and that it was
all part of God's plan for that day. This is where I
have an issue. If we are going to say that the death
of the rescue worker was meant to be, that all things
are destined as God's plan, then why do we have
rescue workers at all? It seems that every time we
have a death or a tragic event, we use the God's plan
phrase to help us feel better. But we are all okay
with sidestepping the "its God's plan" line when it
comes to the "humanitarian" ideals we have
developed, such as using a defibrillator, an epipen,
seat belts, and doing research for finding a cure for
cancer and all the other diseases. We use the "it is
God's plan" only when we benefit from it or can
gain an edge.

I have also noticed that when a person is in a
situation that they feel they are being mistreated or

are being denied a chance to speak on something they feel they should be able to speak on, we are quick to use the term "it is my God given right to…" I am sorry to say this but in no Bible I have read, whether it be the Jewish, the Christian, or the Muslim, have I read where God gave anyone any "rights to talk". The only right God gave us was the right to choose, otherwise worded as freewill. Other than that, the only thing God gave us was obligations. When it comes to "rights" that comes only from our U.S. Constitution. So when it comes to abortion, it seems to be another one of the times that we are picking and choosing when to "use" God as a tool. As for the use of God in the abortion debate it is also a misuse of any of the biblical texts. In each of the three books, the teachings are that each person is responsible for his/her choices and that while it is a person's responsibility to help guide the other, ultimately each person is responsible for his/her actions. So, religion on the surface sounds good and is great for making a person feel guilty about the issue, in reality, it has no place in the abortion issue.

From the legal standpoint, the medical reasoning is the soundest reasoning for establishing abortion parameters. However, I do not feel they are sound enough to establish a complete ban, and therefore making all abortions illegal. What I do see is a valid reason to ban abortions based on the term of the pregnancy; the later into the term, the more legal the ban. However, the most recent arguments have people pushing that conception is now the point of life, and therefore, there can and should be no abortion. This view is taking us back to the religious view only aspect again and I have made my argument on that point already.

Therefore, I see that the use of religion as a reason to ban abortion is invalid, and the medical reasoning is the most sound. I do not see where or why we are still making this an issue. A woman has rights and they need to be respected up until the medical reasoning can take over.

However, there is another issue at play here and that is the rising push to ban all contraceptives as well. When these issues, abortion and contraceptives, are looked at separately, they are fine. But, when you put them together with the base of the argument being rooted into the religious base, we have another issue. We have what I see as a much bigger issue. And if I am right, this would be the most deplorable underhanded scheme yet.

Here is my observation. Some people want to ban abortion. It does not matter to them the justification of it; they just want it banned period. Now, they are pushing to ban contraceptives also. Again, they are pushing under religious grounds right now, but if that does not work, they will try another reason. The new angle is to stop insurance companies from paying for contraceptives, and again, they just want them banned.

But I see an underlying reason, but first let's do a little math. What segment of our population utilizes birth control the most? Yes, it is the white population. If only by sheer numbers, the white population uses birth control the most. Next what segment has the most abortions? Yes you are right again, the white population. While the black population has a higher percentage of abortions per capita, the white population has the highest numbers.

Now I am going to get ugly, but like I have said, I am not into telling people what they want to hear but rather what they need to hear. So if the following gets you a little on edge, I do apologize but I have to bring this point of view to the table. If I am wrong, which I hope and pray that I am, that is fine, but if I am right, oh boy, I don't know what to say. So here we go. IF we banned contraceptives, more women would get pregnant; again there are more white women at this time in this country than any other race, so more white women by numbers would be getting pregnant. Now, we have also banned abortion so what does this mean. On the surface, it means we would be having a huge population explosion, but underneath it would be the solution to what population forecasters are calling a shift in the racial make-up of this country. Think about it. If contraceptives are banned and abortion is banned, the white population would end up holding on to the majority for a much longer amount of time.

I will agree this does sound like a far-fetched notion, but if I can see the dots, who is to say those dots were not laid out hoping nobody would see them? Personally, I pray I am wrong, but I think this is something that should not be ignored. Then you add in one more observation. It is the same people that are arguing to ban abortion on the point that they are saving lives are denouncing the effects humans are responsible for on climate change. The connection here is; climate change is a threat that could possibly wipe out up to a billion lives but the "Pro-lifers" only argue to save lives before they are born. That also makes me wonder what their real motives are on this issue.

Chapter 12

Same Sex marriage

The issue of same sex marriage should be closed just as the abortion issue should be closed now that the Supreme Court has made its' ruling. However, it is clear from the actions of the county clerk in Kentucky that this issue will continue to be an issue for some people. This is another issue that is rooted in religious beliefs and practices.   In reality, religion has no place in this issue, because this issue has nothing to do with religion.

If you take a step back and look at these issues with an open mind you would be able to see the modern day comparison here with the same mindset that justified the political acceptance of the "Jim Crow Laws" that brought down the progress of equality during the reconstruction era in the late 1800's

The current argument maintains that "Marriage is between one man and one woman," when in fact that is not that case. I have read the New Testament and the Old Testament from cover to cover at least ten times, and nowhere can I find there to be a definition or a description of marriage. I have also asked several religious leaders and they either agreed with me, or disagreed but could not give me a chapter or verse to confirm. What I do find in the Bible in regard to marriage are inferences as to how a marriage make up could be. That being, that there is one man and as many wives as he wanted. Jacob had twelve wives while Jesus had none. As for the practice of same sex relations, the New Testament does not talk about it; it only makes reference back to the "Law" which means Leviticus of the Old Testament. In Leviticus, it says that it is an abomination to lay down with a man as if he were a woman, but it makes no reference to woman/woman relations.

As for the New Testament on this matter, like I said, it actually makes no direct reference. What it does say is that Jesus spoke of living your life in a Godly way and not to judge other people. So the way I see this is that religion and the practice of religious or "a spiritual life" is to live life in a way that would make other people want to be like you. Nowhere in the Bibles does it condone the practice of belittling or denial. In fact, Jesus did just the opposite. On the times that he feed the multitudes, he never once said only the believers were welcome to eat; no, never. In the Old Testament it says time after time that "You are to treat the stranger among you the same as you treat a believer." Here, my point is that when people say they are "Believers" and then deny, ridicule, belittle or cast shame on another person because they are living their life in a different way, then the "believer" is doing just the opposite of what is taught in any of the Bibles. The old adage of "You get more bees with honey than you do with vinegar," holds true in religion as well. For me, seeing the behavior of the Kentucky clerk was sad, for this behavior was not Godly, nor did it fit the WWJD program. Jesus walked and talked forgiveness and acceptance. If you will remember, the only mention of him getting angry was when he was in the Temple and saw the practices of the Temple leader being in contrast to the teaching of the Torah. He found that to be hypocritical. On this issue, we are working along the same line of hypocrisy,

In no way am I saying that same sex relationships are proper or, I'll even go as far as saying normal, but that should not be the point here. It is a given that the relationships are not normal, for they cannot create offspring and offspring is the core purpose of life, for without it there is no future. God's first commandment was to go forth and populate; it seems that is the only commandment we all agree to adhere to. (Humor) But hay, with our current trend of world over population growth, maybe we should be happy we have a growing number of same-sex relationships. (Humor)

These same sex relations are not asking for the same benefits that come from a traditional church sponsored marriage. They simply want the same benefits that come from a government sponsored marriage; tax deductions, medical and so on.

They are asking for equal benefits and I am okay with that, but I am also okay with equal practice in other areas as well. There are no heterosexual rallies or parades, so there should be no homosexual parades either. I feel that our government officials should be responsible for preforming the matrimonial ceremonies. I do not believe a religious official that bases his practice out of a Bible that he/she believes to say this practice is wrong should have to perform the weddings. Just because the same-sex couple has rights, their rights do not trump those of people that work in a Bible based church. The government officials do not work under the same principles as the church officials, thus, they should be responsible for performing the ceremonies.

Furthermore, I do not agree with the argument that this is a state's rights issue. I have a friend, and have heard others make the argument that we are a democracy and these issues should be voted on. However, I believe without hesitation or reservation, that this is one of those issues that needs to be universal in all states. This cannot be an issue left up to the voters in each state. This is an issue that goes against the norms of developed culture. This is an issue that puts the practices or rights of a small number of people against the thoughts and feelings of a large number of people. For this issue to be decided on by the voters would be like having a high school football team pitted against the New England Patriots; they have no chance to win. A prime example here would be that if the Civil Rights had been decided by a popular vote, we would still have separate drinking fountains, blacks not allowed in restaurants or in the same school as a white child. You all know this is true. No, this is one of those issues that the federal government has to step in and make sure the rights of all the people are respected as equal no matter what state we live in.

This is also the very reason judges are appointed and not voted in. A judge has the responsibility of deciding what is best for all of the people of this country without fear of retribution or retaliation from any one in any way. A judge has the responsibility of making all the hard calls. In every case he/she handles, one side will be affected in a positive way while the other in a negative way. If the judges were voted in, the decisions they are asked to make would be tainted with the threat of unemployment. This threat by the voters could be called a form of terroristic threatening from the voters. "Make your judicial decisions so that they please me or I will fire you." Again if back in the 1950's and 1960's, judges were living with this type of "threat of re-election" we would still be a legally segregated country.

Bottom line is that we can't care about any couples sexual practice, what people do in their private life, or what position they do it in is nobody's business but their own. What we must care about is interpersonal practice, respect and accountability. If you have those we will get along just fine. Again we are right back to the purity that is at the core of the pledge of allegiance.

...indivisible, liberty and justice for all.

Chapter 13

Religion

I can sum up this section in one line - religion is good, it is the people that practice religion that create the problems.

The following is an explanation of this thought. I will give notice at this time; this topic will produce some **very controversial** thoughts, but they are thoughts that need to be shared. I say this because I know I am not the only person with these thoughts but in almost all cases, people don't express them. They feel they can't express them because our society has developed into such a religious sensitive one that people now feel that the mere speaking on the subject can or will cause such devastatingly, disastrous, polarizing effects on their lives that they choose to keep their mouth shut rather than take the chance on losing their job, their home, or worse.

Furthermore, I have found that I am spending more time on this chapter than any of the others, for two reasons; one, because as controversial as the subject of religion is, I actually love this subject. Two; because while I was doing research for this subject, I actually encountered a number of people that did not know that Jesus was Jewish, two of them vehemently argued he was not Jewish and would not even take the time to talk with me about it. So with that in mind, I decided it might be better to add more to this chapter rather than less.

My thoughts on religion are that religion is both the most unifying as well as the most polarizing entity in human history. Religion has been the cornerstone in many people's lives. It gave them the strength or direction for becoming a better person than they would have been without it. On the other hand, religion has also been the root cause of many people's deaths, even the sole justifier for slavery and even genocide in some cases. When religion is taken simply on its surface messages, religion can be a very calming and beautiful thing; on the other hand, if you live solely by the deeper meanings that have been developed, religion can be a very dark and gruesome way of life. However, when people are able to meld together the right amount of surface and under the surface, or deeper messages, religion can be the greatest tool in helping humanity achieve its greatest highest. The problem is, finding that melding point.

The first and biggest question on the topic of religion is, is there a God? Some people say there is no proof; therefore, if you can't prove there is a God, then there is not one. They say "Get back to me when you have something definitive, meanwhile leave me alone let me live my life as I want." Other people say that there is proof, just look around; everything you see and can't see is proof that there is a God. As for my thoughts? I grew up in a home that did not push religion. While I am Jewish, I was not raised in the Jewish life. My parents felt that religion was something they did not wanted to force on their children. Thus most of my exposure to religion as a child was in the Catholic/Christian faith(s). I did not decide to focus on my Jewish life until well into my adult years. It was after years of education, both formal and non-formal; that I became convinced there was a God. The more science I studied, the more real God became, and once I had my first child, there was no question.

However, I, like my parents, did not push religion on my children. It was not until my son was about to have his first child that I shared this view with him:

One day my son told me he was not all that convinced that there was a God.

I smiled and replied, "I understand your point. I have those thoughts some days too, but let me ask you, why you are feeling this way?"

He said, "Well it just does not make sense, if there was a God why would he/she not tell us, why would it not be clear?"

I again smiled and looked at him and said, "You are about to have your first child, the journey you are about to begin will be one of the most fascinating times of your life. Watching your child grow up will be a twofold fascination."

1. One you will get a firsthand idea of just what it is like to be a God, meaning your daughter is going to look at you as if you are a God. That is because to her, in her eyes and in her life, at least until she is about 7, she will think and believe you are indeed a God, her God. All the things

you will be doing, you will provide her food and clothes, more so you will be the one that provides her with all her learning and her loving. You will be the one that is there for her when she falls down and scrapes her knee, and when she gets sick, you will be the one that holds her. She will look into your eyes and there is no explaining that feeling, only a parent knows. But I will tell you, it will be at these times that you will know that she will be looking at you as a God, her God, and you will again get to wonder, is there a God?

2. As well there will be another angle. Every day you will be so amazed at watching her grow and develop, seeing her little fingers and toes grow, and knowing that all the tiny organs inside her are all working, developing and growing in a way that no scientist can even come close to duplicating. Yes, you will start to think about the possibility of there being a God.

So I said again; you are about to have your first child, let's re-visit this discussion again when your baby is about 3 years old

His response was, well dad I am really thinking that the amoeba theory of evolution fits pretty well.

I said, yes I can see your point, but let's look at that a little further;

1. Once the earth was created (oops I mean developed) and after a couple million years pass by, a little bitty single cell amoeba jumps out of the ocean, lands on the beach and decided to evolve into a billion cell organism called a human.

2. Okay, well while that sounds all good, what is the mathematical chances of that happening. Keeping in mind that somehow it seems that nearly every animal life form on this planet has relatively the same digestive system, circulatory system, nervous system and cardiovascular system.

3. However, there is more to think on this; keep in mind there wasn't just one little single cell amoeba that jumped out of the sea that day, there had to be at least two. There had to be one that developed into a female while the other a male, both showing up on the same beach at the same time in the billions of year(s) that Earth has been around so the human evolution could get going.

4. Ad why are they not continuing to jump out of the sea and evolve?
5. Furthermore, keep in mind there is much more to think about than the simple evolving humanoid on the beach. There is also the continued survival of the human race. Meaning on this, think about how long it takes for a human child to become not just self-aware but to be self-sufficient, to the point where its parents would be able to go hunt and or gather food for its survival.

All he did was give me a raised eyebrow and a deep "Hum"

The question of whether there is a God or not will be an ongoing thing, and I for one hope and pray that the question will never be answered. This is my reasoning. If we find out without question that there is a God, then all the challenge, or what some call fun of life, will be gone. Meaning, if God comes along and sets us all straight on this issue, then we will no longer have the "Free will" that we were given in the book of Genesis. We have to be honest here; the best part of life is the challenge of free will. If God were here, then the entire unknown would be gone. We would not have to deal with any lies that people may tell. We would not get the stressful frustration out of having to choose which television show to watch, if we got to watch TV at all. I for one cherish my freedom of choice as well as everyone else's. I love the challenge of waking up every day and putting together my daily plan of motivation. I enjoy planning out what I am going to do to make sure my life, as well as at least one other person's life is better by the end of that day. I love going to bed every night asking myself what I could have done better that day and how I could improve upon that tomorrow. However, if God were in fact on this planet, all that would be gone, life would simply be a day after day of simply getting up, smile at people and going to bed waiting for it all to end. No, my thoughts are that the chase for heaven is what makes life fun.

I have a view on the choice of "temptation" being a necessary part of life. Some say that if a person thinks about doing something bad, it as if they actually did it; thus, a negative thought is already a guilty act. I have a different view. I view that negative thoughts are just what God wants us to have. They are a must for people to earn their right into heaven. The following is how I explain this;

I have a child and I am teaching him/her the difference between right and wrong. I am teaching him that the difference between right and wrong all hinges on the choices she makes. One day, I see my child go into the kitchen. I notice that it is just before dinner, so I peak around the corner to watch what she is up to. I see he is about to reach for the cookie jar. This is something we had been working on, no eating before dinner. So I watch with baited breath, she reaches up, opens the lid, reaches in, and then stops. There is a pause and he brings his hand back out with no cookie. He turns and leaves the kitchen empty handed. As the father of this child, I am filled with pride and joy as a big smile comes over my face. As well, an exuberant fist pump is exercised as I realize my child is indeed developing the ability to make that right choice.

This is the simplistic example of what God does every day as he watches each and every one of us. It is either the jubilation dance or it is a disgruntled look with a head shake of disappointment knowing that the bad choice we just made shows we are not quite ready to be trusted being left alone just yet.

On the other hand, if it were to be proven that there is no God, life would be chaos. There would or could be no enforceable laws; all law and order as we know it would be gone. Life would truly be the survival of the fittest. I say this because, without the moral hope that comes with the faith of there being a God, for the vast majority of the people, there is no reason to be civilized.

However, with religion being very broad and in many ways vague, it leaves open the opportunity to be misused, misapplied and/or misinterpreted. Therefore, people or governments guided by religion can lead to major atrocities for all the wrong reasons. We read about this in our history books and we see it still today in some countries. What I mean by this is that people can/have/do actually live their lives in a way that they truly believe is right by the Bible without noticing how their ways/beliefs/practices are actually counterproductive to the overall message of the Bible. The following is an example from my life; I was married to a lady for seven years, and we were friends for two years prior. She was a raised but not practicing Pentecostal Christian lady, a nice girl that I loved and cared for deeply. One day, nine years into our relationship, we were sitting in the living-room talking about the possible future of our son.

There we were, sitting there two young parents talking about our son's future life choices. The topic comes to dating, specifically him bringing a date home from college for a weekend or so. As we talked about this we, were both ok with him bringing a date home. However, we started to differ from each other when it came to the option of him dating interracially. She was fine with him having a date but they would not be allowed to sleep in the same room. Me, I figured why not, if they were sleeping together in their own world, why force them to be different. Her thoughts were, that if they are not married then they cannot sleep together; it is a sin and it says so in the Bible. I was a bit shocked to be hearing this since she had never brought up "The Bible" before. Furthermore, my feelings were, why make it an issue, all we would be doing in the long run was creating a rift between him and us. Besides, she and I had slept together before we were married. But to me that was not that big of an issue at that time and really did not think much of it. However, the parameters changed slightly when I said. "Well what if his girlfriend is black?" Keep in mind we were a white couple. Oh boy, did it get heated from there. After being together for about nine years at this time, I learned something that night that I never thought or dreamed possible about this lady.

Her words got loud and stern when she said, "Oh no, he will not have a black girlfriend." I asked, "Why?" She said, "It is just wrong!" "How is it wrong?" I asked. She said, "It is in the Bible, blacks are to stay with their kind and whites to theirs." When I pointed out that I didn't see anything wrong with it, she got furious. And said, "Well if he grows up and dates a n&%er I will not have anything to do with him." I laughingly said, "Are you serious?" She replied she was. I then broke down some specific situations to her; I asked, "Are you telling me, if he is dating a lady that is educated, works a good job, takes care of him, keeps the house clean, cooks and does everything right for him, but she was black, you would not want to be around him." She said. "Yes, that is correct." I then said, "So you would be ok if he was with and uneducated, dirty lady that did not work or clean or anything like that but she was white, you would be ok with her, is that what you are saying." She replied with a resounding, "YES!"

I had never dreamed she had these thoughts or ideals in her, but she based them off her religious upbringing. Nine years and I had never heard anything about her bible views or that she had these deeply rooted racial segregationist views like this. Well, that made a big difference to me, because I could not just let that slide as I could with the topic of just not being allowed to sleep with his girlfriend. Now I saw a double standard in two areas; one, to make it simple, she was 5 months pregnant when we got married. So it was okay for us to sleep together before being married but she was not going to let her son. That was what I called an acceptable hypocritical view that I felt would change by the time we got to that point. However, now came the adamant position of a double standard based on color, and that I could not accept.

Yet it got even worse for me, I asked her, "Okay what if he brings home another man?" WOW, did she go off. She actually got up out of her chair and through her arms up and said, "Oh no, there is no way my son is going to be gay." I said, "Well if he is, there is nothing you can do about that, if he is, he is." She said, "NO, if he grows up gay I will kill myself!" Again I was shocked to hear her say this. I asked, "Are you serious, you would actually do that to him?" She said, "Do what; I did not do anything; if he is gay that is his fault." I said, "No, I mean, if he is gay and you kill yourself because of that, do you realize the guilt he will have to live with." Her reply, "Was that is not my fault he should not have been gay, the Bible says you cannot be gay, I cannot and will not live with that."

This was a conversation that happened in January of 1993 and I remember it as if it was just an hour ago. It was that night that I realized this relationship could not continue. I knew when we got together what her religious background was, but I did not know the full extent of her religious beliefs. I filed for divorce one month later, and was granted full custody when it was all over.

It is those very core beliefs that I am talking about when I say people do bad things because of religion that they truly feel is/are the right things to do. I know my son's mother did not at that time see anything wrong with her views, nor does she today, they have only gotten stronger. She felt then as she does still today that her views are correct and healthy because that is what she learned in her bible studies. My son's mother grew up in the south while I grew up in the north. She grew up going to church every day, I did not. I personally think I ended up with healthier views, but I might be a bit biased on that point.

We were just one couple, and that was just one event in our lives in which I saw how the effects of religious beliefs can have a negative impact or outcome, even though the person truly believes that they are doing nothing wrong or harmful to anyone, and in fact they think they are doing the right thing by God, based on the way they were taught.

Religious teachings are the way we are taught our "Moral beliefs and practices," but just because we are teaching things or establishing laws or policies based on religion make them right. There are countless times that people have done heinous crimes in the name of religion. As well teaching our religious morals as we do, and engraining them into our laws we are creating people to become criminals that would have otherwise done nothing wrong. An example of this is: In Louisville Kentucky 2015 there was a young teenage girl visiting her grandmother I the hospital. While there she gave birth to a child in a restroom and hid the baby. The baby was found alive and the girl was ultimately found as well. The young teenage girl was arrested and charged with several felony charges.

This girl was not a criminal, she was simply a young scared child that made decisions based on shame, religiously rooted shame. This girl is not a criminal, she is a victim. She is a victim of an over moralistic society. This girl was raised in a society that said underage sex was wrong; she was raised in a society that said unwed pregnancy was a violation of Gods laws. This young child was living in a society that had the medical technology that could help her but that same society not only denied her the medical help, it actually added to her shame. Our society now focuses using abortion as a moral weapon against women's' freedom. This young girl in Louisville Kentucky lived a life no different than thousands of other young girls. This young girl lives in a society that is using the threat of moral shame to prevent wrong doing. This young girl is not a criminal for this situation; it is our society that is wrong here.

This girl, like millions of other teenagers experimented with sex, and that experiment led to a situation this child was unable to talk with her parents about; again it is because of the high level of moral shame that comes with teenage pregnancy in our society. It is also clear this girl; the same as countless other girls in our country was not able to use the Planned Parenthood system either, again do to the moral shame that comes with doing so if they are found to have done so. Therefore, this girl like all the other girls in her situation are forced, out of moral shaming to keep these pregnancies to themselves and ultimately end up like this young lady, branded a criminal, having to live with a felony record for the rest of their lives. This is my biggest concern on our country's focus on moral standards based on religious interpretations. At this level we are not only driving people away from religion we are also taking innocent young kids and making them out to be criminals for simply doing a natural human instinct. An act that according to the Bible was the first commandment given to Adam and Eve; Go Forth and Multiply. However, we also have to keep in mind all through the Bible we are told to have compassion on others. There is no stipulation as to the others are, it does not say have compassion on those that think like you, act like you or believe like you. No the book says we are to have compassion on others. Therefore, I say we can continue to teach the moral ethics but learn to have compassion on others. This does not mean turn a blind eye to crime or bad behavior, but rather be compassionate, understanding and willing to work with people until they show us they are not willing to work within the laws of morality. Yet, we also have to take into consideration the people on the other end of the morally shamed pendulum. We have people that have lived their lives having the religious morals drummed into them to the point that they lose touch with the civil society and end up killing people on the belief they are doing right be God as they have been taught. Again while I believe religion is a good thing, we have to admit it does have its drawbacks.

However, living in the United States, with the Constitution that we have, it becomes very confusing as to just what role religion can or should play in our society. I say this because, while the Bill of Rights, First Amendment states;

Congress shall make no law respecting an establishment of religion, or prohibiting the free exercise thereof;

Just what this wording means is not clear, thus we have had hundreds of cases go (gone) before the U.S. Supreme Court that have had this very issue at their root. This makes it clear that religion plays a major role in all parts of our lives. Whether a person practices Monotheism, Polytheism, is an Atheist, or fits into any other religious/spiritual niche, there can be no question that religion plays a major role in your lives.

This issue, as to how much of a factor religion should legally fit into our lives, becomes even more confusing when you read the Declaration of Independence and the original Constitution. You see that the "framers" themselves made reference to a creator, and as well, made usage of the word God, specifically in the closing of the Constitution it states "In the year of our Lord..." Therefore, it seems we have a dilemma of a "do as I say, not as I do" situation. The framers' actions, by way of their written words, tend to show that they were arguably religious/spiritual men. Yet, before the ink had dried on the Constitution, they were already penning the aforementioned first amendment.

I now propose that the framers use of references to Our Lord, God, and the Creator are all superficial uses and only in place for formal image purposes. We all know of people that do this, speak with godly overtones but walk around the corner to the local bar and talk trash while they pick a fight with the first person that looks at them in a wrong way. You see, these references were used at the beginning of our fight for freedom, at the penning of the Declaration of Independence, at a time when people were in a desperate mode, at a time when people needed hope. Hope then, just as now, is best bolstered by interjecting God into the equation. Thus, the injection of the wording

"...Laws of Nature and of Nature's God entitle them..." Followed shortly by *"...that all men are created equal, that they are endowed by their Creator with certain unalienable Rights, that among these are Life, Liberty and the pursuit of Happiness...",*

Into the Declaration of Independence, were all meant to rally the people with hope. Then, the use of the wording "in the year of our Lord" at the ending of the Constitution were simply words of formality.

Now, let's take a look at other written actions in the Constitution. After the penning of "all men are created equal" in the Declaration of Independence to rally the peoples' emotions against the British to whom they felt were oppressing them, they then wrote in the actual; section 2 paragraph 3 that *non free men were to be counted as just three fifths of a man,* and then in section 9 paragraph 1,

The Migration or Importation of such Persons as any of the States now existing shall think proper to admit, shall not be prohibited by the Congress prior to the Year one thousand eight hundred and eight, but a Tax or duty may be imposed on such Importation, not exceeding ten dollars for each Person.

This is to acknowledge the practice of slavery, but yet, never abolish it. So I say, the actions of their writings in the constitution are not consistent with the wording of *"all men are created equal...,* and that the first amendment barring the injection and/or infusion of religion into our politics is more in step with their ideals of their words, rather than their actions and/or practices.

It took until 1865; some 87 years, or four score and seven years (Oh I am sorry that is another speech on this subject...) and a civil war to finally get that Constitutional wrong corrected. Even then, many people were not/are not willing to accept that ALL people are capable of being equal. I truly feel that the framers missed out on a great opportunity. My "thoughts" are that they set the mindset of innate inequality with this action at that time. Had they abolished slavery in the original writing of the Constitution, it would have set a whole different example for all the people in this country. This simple action would have prevented the Civil War, the reconstruction period, the Jim Crow laws, and millions of lost lives. It would have eliminated the need for the Civil Rights Acts of the 1950's and 1960's, but that is just my thoughts.

This very set of actions and lasting results/effects show my very point as to just how important, powerful and influential religion can be. In the hands, the hearts and the minds of some people, religion can be a very helpful, if not a necessary tool that helps to make people not only healthier, but also into a stronger, and better humanity. While on the other hand, religion to some can and is used as a powerful weapon, a very powerful and deadly weapon. Our world history is riddled with documented events in which mass killings were carried out under the auspices of religion. Examples include present day Middle East Muslims, Jim Jones, The KKK movement, the Jim Crowe laws, the U.S. practice of slavery, the hundreds of years of Crusades, Spanish Inquisition and least I not mention the event which is arguably the most talked about of all time, that being the Biblical event of the crucifixion of Jesus. All of these events have cost the lives of millions of people, not to mention their potential offspring, and these are only but a few in our history. However, the biggest thing about each and every one of these events is to remember that all the people were acting on what they truly believed was the right thing based on their religious teachings and understandings at that time. Again, I only point these out as examples of how religion can and has been used in a negative way or has been a detriment to some/many people over the course of time.

These are all historical events that were caused by the extremist practices of religion or the misinterpretation of the Biblical text. It was not religion itself, but rather it was the acts of the people that interrupted the religious message that carried out these events. What makes this worse is that the vast majority of the people that participate(ed) in these events were being told to do so by their "religious leader(s) that were telling them just what God meant when He wrote the Biblical text. In most cases the religious leader ended up being what we now dub a "Fanatical Religious Leader," or "an extremist." This was made possible because in each one of these events of fanatical, religious extremist genocides, the literacy rate was very low. When people can't read they are left to the mercy of those that can, and most people want to trust and believe that their religious leaders would tell them the truth and not mislead them.

As I pen these words, I know there is an extremist, fanatical religious group that is taking someone's life in the name of God somewhere in the world. The sad but honest truth is, not a single one of the three major religions at bar are without shame. While all three of the major religions, Jewish, Christian and Islam have the same root, the same core beliefs and practices, none of them can come up with a way to accept each other and work together as a whole for the betterment of all. Each of these religions is rooted in and from Abraham whose story is told in the book of Genesis. For the Jewish and Christians, this is in the Old Testament, or as I refer to it, The Original Testament, and in the Quran; Surah xiv (Ibrahim) for the Muslims. Each of these religions has the same underlining core belief; that is to make the world a better place to live. In each religion, it gives specific directions, rules, requests, or commandments that say people are first and foremost supposed to LOVE each other, love their neighbor, and love their brother... While each does say you may kill, each also says you are not to murder, Leviticus for the Jewish and Christians and Surah xvii (Israelites) for Islam. They all give examples of what constitutes the difference between killing and murder. Killing is only justified when you are defending yourself or justified honor, while murder is killing out of rage or out of hate. The biggest thing here, in each religion, it is clear that God, no matter what name you use, is the same God for all the Jewish people, all the Christians and all the Muslims; they all have the same God, "The God of Abraham." More importantly in each book, it makes it clear that you shall put no God before this God. For the Jews and Christians, it is in Exodus and Leviticus, and for Islam, it is in Surah xvii (Israelites). The key thing in each of these books and in the way each of them is written, it is clear that all of them say "You shall have/place no other god before me" in these rules that are written by "The God." What this clearly means is that the God that wrote these rules does say clearly that there are and will be other gods, in and around the world, and you can have them, BUT, just make sure you do not put them before or above Him/Her. This is not that hard to understand but for some reason it is a major hostility point in each and every one of these religions for some reasons.

The Jewish peoples are people that are in the life/practice/faith of Judaism by way of family bloodline or through a lengthy educational and ceremonial conversion process. The Jewish faith is the only religion that once you are in, you can't get out. Meaning, once you are born in, or convert in you will always be Jewish. It does not matter if you are a good Jew or a bad Jew; it does not matter if you practice or not. As a matter of fact, it doesn't even matter if you start practicing another religion, you are still Jewish, and there is no de-conversion from Judaism. The Jewish people, or the Nation of Israel are by Biblical record the first born religion of "The God of Abraham," there is no definitive birthday for this religion. Is it the beginning of creation (Hebrew calendar 5775) or is it the date of Abraham's birth? Or, is it the year of his circumcision? Or, was it the year that he was given the blessing of his son, Isaac? Or, was it the year that Moses brought the nation of Israel out of Egypt? Or, was it the day that God gave the Torah to the people of Israel? However, from whatever year is decided they are still the oldest, and for a time in "BCE" were the only one of these religions and were not above these extremist fanatical behaviors

However, a group of Rabbis came up with a radical idea and started pushing the idea of reading for everyone. (The first implementation of the "No child left behind plan.") This made it to where everyone was capable of reading the Torah (Jewish bible, otherwise known as the "Old Testament" or as I call it, The Original Testament) for themselves. From that point it became each person's responsibility to read, study, understand and live the life they interpreted from their own readings. So, it was the act of literacy and education for all the people, men, women and children that was the key to survival of the minority without being the aggressor, the dominant one, or better said survival without being the fittest. It was the act of teaching literacy skills which allowed the people to understand their Bible and then be able to think for themselves that was able to cut out the extremist actions. However, over time the people of the Jewish faith started having differences of opinions on how practices and policies should go, so they have now split into three separate categories, Orthodox, Reform and Conservative. This split has occurred within the last 200 years and was more of a development of growth then it was a split. There were no hostile feelings or violent revolt between the Jewish people that caused the development of the new Jewish practices. Rather the Jewish people realized that they needed to assimilate their religion somewhat in order to survive. The first side group to develop was the reform; they made some drastic changes to the practice in an attempt to appease the Christian majority that was in power. In a short period of time, about fifty years the changes had become so drastic that a number of "Reform Jews" decided things had gone too far. They did not want the old school ways of the Orthodox but they were not comfortable with the excessive relaxing for the new Reform branch. So they created the third Jewish branch, they would be called the Conservative Jews. The Jewish faith is thousands of years old, as I said it is the first one of the three religions brought forth by Abraham yet it was the last one to split or develop multiple branches, but it is important to say there is no animosity between the different branches. I personally relate mostly with the Conservative branch but I attend a Reform Temple because the Rabbis at that Temple are so nice, so thoughtful and so passionate about the faith and the people in their congregation that I am very happy staying right where I am at.

Today the Jewish religion is the smallest in population by way of numbers of the three religions. The Jewish people are scattered all over the world, yet each one is always on the same page as the others when it comes to the studies and religious messages. There is a set schedule of Biblical reading that is read each week of the year. This is good because this makes it so if a Jewish person is traveling anywhere in the world, they will always be at home in any synagogue or Temple they chose to stop into along their way.

My personal favorite verse in the Torah – Original Testament – Old Testament is; Leviticus 19:18 *you shall love your fellow as yourself.*

A side story for this point in time in the Jewish faith, one of the radical Rabbis from back in time was called "Hillel," and I would like to share one of his historical teachings he had with a man:

There was a certain non-Jewish man that came to ask about converting to be Jewish. He asked Hillel to explain to him the principles of the Torah, but could he do it while standing on one leg. Hillel laughed and sent him away, but again the man came back with the same silly request, and again, Hillel sent him off. When the individual came to Hillel on the third occasion with the same request, Hillel responded. "No problem!" Hillel, then standing on one leg said; the main idea of the Torah is, "what is harmful to yourself, do not do to your fellow'(rooted from Leviticus 19:18) everything else is commentary. Now, if you're really interested, go and study the commentary." So impressed with Hillel's response, according to Jewish Tradition, was the visitor, that he took Hillel up on his instructions, began to study the Torah seriously, and became a Jew.

Throughout the Torah, it is commanded time and time again that the Jewish people are to treat the stranger amongst them with love and respect as if he/she was a member of the family. Thus, it is reinforced over and over that you are to treat all people the same. Furthermore, the Jewish calendar is filled with holidays. One specific holiday is called Passover/Pesach. This holiday is 'a mandatory holiday commanded by God to be observed each year in the spring (Hebrew calendar Nisan 14). The whole purpose of this holiday is for all the Jewish people to come together, recite from a book called the Haggadah, at which time we all re-live the days of the bondage in Egypt. The overall theme/message to every person is; not to weep, not cry or feel sorry for the event, but rather to keep this event from our past in the forefront of our lives. With the prime directive being; remember what happened to you and yours and make sure you do not do this to anyone else. The event is to teach us not to dwell on the negatives from past but rather to embrace our past miseries; the purpose is to make the present a better place for everyone.

Granted, the Jewish people still have their share of religious extremists walking around today, it is just fortunate that the mainstream Jewish population is aware of them and is both willing and able to keep them in check.

Next we have the Christian faith, which is people that follow the practices taught through the "New Testament" or "The Holy Bible," which is referred to as the New Covenant." It makes reference back to the Jewish Torah for all their points of law and historical reference. While the Jewish faith is a closed family religion, Christianity is an open to the public religion. What I mean by this is that the Christian faith has no restrictions on who can practice the religion. This religion accepts each and every person to come and join while only asking that each person read the Bible, learn, and then go out into the world and practice the message that Jesus taught. Christianity was born in the first century, "CE," being the second born of the religions from the "God of Abraham." Christianity is a wonderful religion; it is a faith that was developed from the life practices and teachings of a Jewish man named Jesus that many believe to have been the Messiah.

The Christians are also a religion rooted in peace and famous for The Lord's Prayer;

THE LORD'S PRAYER

Our Father who art in heaven, hallowed be thy name. Thy kingdom come, Thy will be done on earth as it is in heaven. Give us this day our daily bread, and forgive us our trespasses, as we forgive those who trespass against us, and lead us not into temptation, but deliver us from evil.

For thine is the kingdom, and the power, and the glory, for ever and ever.

Amen.

And the golden rule – Matthews 7:12

"So whatever you wish that others would do to you, do also to them, for this is the Law of the Prophets."

This verse is referenced from Leviticus 19:18

I have said religion is a powerful thing, in the hands of the right person or people it can be a wonderful tool, but in the wrong hands it can be a disastrous weapon. Like the Jewish people the

Christians also went through a phase of learning how to live peacefully with the religious teachings they were receiving. Nonetheless they too through the act of opening up and allowing literacy to be available to women and children as well as all men, not just the chosen few. Christianity has become a much more open, humane and understanding people. There is little question that Christianity is the largest by numbers of the three major religions. Though the religion as a whole has done remarkable humanitarian things for the whole world, the Christians also still have some fanatical extremists as well; the Westboro Baptist church comes to mind right here at home. However, it must also be noted that there are some extremist Christians on the other end of the spectrum as well; The Amish, the Mennonites, the Brethren Quakers to name just a few. The Christion faith officially got started about eighty years after the death of Jesus (give or take 20 to 30 years). It developed into our present day Catholic faith which lasted about a thousand years before it had its first split. Then about three to four hundred years later the beginning of the Christian splintering started. We now have countless types or categories of the Christian faith.

As a Jewish man, I am frequently asked what my opinion or take is on Jesus, how he fits into my world, with that question at hand, let me share this story with you;

I have a couple of Mormon missionary friends, one in particular that I always referred to him as "EB," they will stop by to talk with me regularly. We have on occasion spent time working together and on every occasion, we always find time to talk about scripture. These men are always the nicest young men a person will ever meet. On one occasion, they finally got around to asking me "The question," meaning what are my thoughts or views on Jesus.

My response was simple, that he is the best Uncle a person could ever ask for.

They looked at each other then turned back to me and asked what I meant by that.

I replied, "As you know Jesus was a Jewish man. In my world he was not the messiah, but he was a very good person, and I think the message that he inspired is great. The message that people should spend their lives doing things in nice and respectful ways for or with other people is a wonderful message. The intended practice of the Christion faith is also a wonderful thing." I went on to tell them that, as for them specifically I felt that the things they were doing while out fellowshipping with people were things they should be proud of, that the behavior and practices that they were displaying were exactly what Jesus was asking people to do.

I explained to them, that they themselves were doing the same things as Jesus did, only in a different era. I told them if in their walks they touch just one person in a positive way, whether that person is old or young, then you have made a difference. That is what Jesus is all about, making a difference, a positive difference. If in any of their encounters they are able to say or do anything to another person that may cause them at some point in their lives to question an action they are about to do, and change the action to a good one, then that is just like my example of my child's actions with the cookie jar. This could be equivalent to a miracle. I say that because; let's say there is a man that is down on his luck. He is having a bad day, has no money, he and his family are hungry, and he sets out to solve this problem by robbing a store to get money to feed him and his family. But, along the way at some point, he thinks about something you guys have told him in your visit, he then changes his mind before entering the store. Now, through your words, you have not only saved that man from committing the crime of robbery, you may have also saved a person's life. Because if the robbery would have went wrong, who knows what might have happened.

We continued to have many talks and some were even over dinner. My wife is a very good cook, and we all enjoy and look forward to the times we have together.

In the Jewish practice, there is a term "Tikkun olam" which means to repair this broken world. This was the basic message in all of Jesus' teachings and that also is exactly what I see so many Christians doing, including the Mormon men. The Christian religion has many people that live and work in the same way as the Mormon men I spoke of. I personally think that the people of the Christian faith have the greatest opportunity to make a difference in improving the Earth. You see, in the Christian faith, there are no prerequisites or hoops for a person to go through to join the religion. With that being the case, the opportunity to have more people in the religion is much greater. The key will be to have more of the people that have accepted the Christian faith for their religion; step up and live the exemplary Christian life. If, and this is a big if, all the Jewish and Christian believers/followers were to actually live the life as scriptures call for, our world would be a much better place. I will say this; I know that if just the Jewish and Christian men and women walked the walk as they are supposed to, the prisons would have a lot less people in them. If the Muslims end up getting their system working like it is promoted to work, well the prisons would be almost empty. That's just my thought on that. I say this because I will guarantee that at least seventy percent of all persons in prison align themselves as being one of the big three religions.

Now we come to my thoughts on Islam, being the third religion born of the "God of Abraham." It is now time to share my thoughts on it. Islam was born in the first decade of the seventh century and is the product of a man named Mohammed, followers of Islam refer to him as The Prophet Mohammed." This religion is referred to the third of the religions born from "The God of Abraham" because Mohammed was a descendent of Ismael, the son of Abraham that was bore to Hagar Abraham's maid-servant. This religion is, at this point the biggest and best example on my point that religion is not bad; it is the people that practice the religion that are the problem. Islam, like Christianity, also has no prerequisites for participation. It is open to anyone that wants to join, read the Quran and follow the teachings.

The book for the Islamic faith is called the Quran, and like the Christian faith, is also based off the Jewish bible. In fact, the first five books of the Jewish Torah are the same books that are the root of the Quran, and are referred to time and time again. As a grown, curious man, I like to read all kinds of books and the Quran happened to be one I decided to read, as did I with the Holy Bible of the Christians, and the Book of Mormon for the Mormons. Furthermore, I took a class at the University of Louisville in the late 1980's titled "Islamic Thought and Culture." My instructor was a lady that grew up in Iran during the years of the "Shah" and was expelled after the revolution in the late 1970's because under the new Ayatollah rules in Iran, women were not allowed to be educated, much less be teachers. I also have several friends that are practicing Muslims and we have regular religious discussions.

As I have said, religion is not the problem; it is the people that practice it that are the problem. Here, I will give an example. Roughly fifteen hundred years ago when Islam was born, it had a much different intent then what its practice is today, or has been for the last century. Prior to Mohammed becoming the Prophet, he was just a regular guy roaming around in the Middle East. He was friends with many Jews as well as Christians; he even studied both religions and was interested in converting to Judaism. But as history shows, he did not. However, never at any time before or after his trip up the mountain for a forty day stay, as Moses did, did he have any issues with either of the other faiths. In fact, he on several occasions he talked to and compared notes sort-a-say with the other religious leaders.

Some of my Muslim friends and I have talked about whether they have ever read the Torah or the bible. One said yes, he had read both. One said he had not read either and two said they had never read the Torah but had read the bible, but it was when they were practicing as Christians before they converted to Islam. Both of those men said that they had been told by their Imam that now that they were Muslims, they were not allowed to read any religious book(s) other than the Quran, I found that a bit harsh. So I went back to "Raj" who was born and raised as a Muslim, yet had told me he had read both the Torah and the Bible. I asked him about how that happened, if you are not to read any other religious books then how or why did you read the Torah and or the Bible. He laughed and said that there was no such true rule in Islam. He said that Islam never 'discourages' a Muslim from reading the Torah because Islam is founded upon the Torah, as is also the case with Judaism and Christianity.

This goes back to my very point that it is the people, not the religion, that are bad. Here it shows that the men that are teaching from the Quran now are doing much the same as the Jewish and Christian faith leaders had done centuries before. It has now been over fifteen hundred years since the death of Mohammed; this is a man that in all his days on earth never did anything, in anyway, whether in his writings, or his words to indicate that he was or should be considered equal to, or on the same level as God. On the contrary, in his lifetime, all he wanted was to give humanity another opportunity to become better humans. He did not want, ask, or expect to be idolized or elevated to the level of a God. Furthermore, he in no way ever wanted or expected people to be killing people in his name. This is a man that went out of his way to make sure there were no picture likenesses made of him during his lifetime. This was not because he wanted to be idolized or elevated to a godly status, on the contrary, in his life he had seen what was becoming of Jesus and his followers. Mohammed saw how the followers of Jesus, by that time the Christians, were using his likeness and creating an image that God was merely a man. This was something Mohammed was adamant he did not want to happen with him and the Islamic faith. He wanted to make sure of that at his passing, and yes he knew he was going to pass, because while people looked at him as a prophet, he knew he was still just a man, and as all men do, he had to pass. While Mohammad wanted and expected the Islamic faith to continue after his passing, he did not intend or want for him and his likeness to be portrayed in such a way that made him equal to or on the same level as a God. However, over the years, this is exactly what has happened.

This now brings us to something that needs to be asked about present day Islam. It is written that Islam was brought to Muhammad because at the time the following was being said;

"It is said that the Torah is true but men have distorted the words and meaning of the Torah."

This question is what was being said at the time of Islam's birth, that being. I now pose that very point again; the book (Quran) is good; it is the people that have now over the years distorted the words and meanings of the Islamic religion. We now have some people of Islam known as Muslims that are killing other people under the premise of defending the honor of the prophet Muhammad. In 2015, there was a killing by some Muslim men in the country of France at a newspaper office because the newspaper had printed cartoons about the prophet Muhammad. Thus, the men believed they were in the right to kill in order to protect the honor of the prophet. However, this was not a killing, this was murder. While I may not be the first one to say the killing was wrong, I will probably be one of the first one to explain why it was wrong. This explanation will be a multi-pronged explanation. While the Torah and Bible say in the Ten Commandments; you shall not kill, the Torah and Quran say you can kill but you cannot murder. That while killing has justifications based of self-defense or through a line of defending yours or a person's honor it is okay, but outside of that it is wrong and called murder. It is a condemned act by all religions. Furthermore, when a person kills under the false premise of honor just to kill someone, that is truly wrong and that is also murder. I now say that all the killings that have been done and are being done under the auspice of avenging the honor of the Prophet Muhammad are in fact, based on the Quran and the historical practices of Muslims, are indeed all murders.

As previously established for the Torah and Holy Bible, the Quran does in fact state "you are to love your brother/neighbor as you would love yourself. And that God does not love the man that is proud or stingy." (Surah 4 – 36). I now state that any man that is willing to kill another person based on the "honor" theory of a man that said in his own writings, in his own time, that he was nothing more than a messenger of God and was not to be seen as a God in any way. If any person that uses the honor of the prophet as their justification for killing is doing so because of their pride. They are so proud of Muhammad that they are killing to protect his image, an image that he himself shunned. This person is now killing out of pride, and therefore is in direct violation of the teachings of the Quran, not of Sharia law, but of the Quran itself. Thus, it makes these killings all murder, and they need to stop.

The Quran also says time after time all throughout that a believer (a practicing Muslim) is to live his/her life the right way and be an example to others as to how to live. Furthermore, it clearly states that you (as a believer) are to stay clear and far away from the non-believers or wrong doers. Nowhere does it say anyone is to kill/murder another person just because they do not follow the ways of Islam. On the contrary, it says time after time that God has a plan for the non-believers. Again, that God has a plan; not that you are to have a plan, but God has one.

Furthermore, the Quran is filled with points that say God is God and that no one is equal to God, and that includes Muhammad. It does make reference to Angles and in some parts is written in third person text, but still always maintains that God is God and there is no equal. In fact, it continuously states that God has made some people bad and that God will deal with those people at the appropriate time. Nowhere in the Quran does it say that the Prophet Muhammad or any other prophet is on the equal plane as God, and therefore carries the same homage when it comes to defending "Their honor."

Muhammad asked that there be no pictures of him made, not to protect his honor, but rather to protect God's honor. This is because, as I stated, Muhammad saw what was happening to the Christian religion by having images of Jesus, that being, that people were putting more reverence to the "man" of Jesus than they were to the God, and he did not want that effect to happen with Islam. He felt that if people had his image and were honoring that image of him, which in fact would take honor away from God. So what indeed has happened is in fact, just the opposite of what the prophet wanted.

People are now killing people in the name of defending the prophet's honor, when in fact he wanted no honor like this. He was a humble man that wanted all people to know that God deserved to have the entire honor.

Thus, people that are killing in the name of defending his honor in a picture are in fact actually dishonoring the prophet by killing in his name. Thus, all these killings are murders and by the words of the Quran itself, this is wrong. So killing in the name of defending the prophet's honor is in fact dishonoring to God, so now who is the in violation?

I further support my point by using Muslim historical practice. Let's keep in mind we are talking about the year 630ish AD. There were not a lot of cameras being sold at the local market, so we can accept that pictures of any sort were not hanging around on every wall. In fact, historically throughout the world, middle-east included, the way people were honored was through the naming of children, and that still holds true today. Children were taught to behave in accordance with respect for their namesake. That being, the most common name in the Muslim world is Muhammad. With that being the fact, I say; if the prophet was worried about being dishonored or insulted he would have banned his name from being given to others. I say this because it proves my point that Muhammad's request to not have pictures was not to preserve his honor but that of God's honor. Muhammad maintained that all honor is to go to God and not him; thus, he did not want people seeing a picture of him and thinking that was a picture of God, as was happening in the Christian religion. It was not to save face from ridicule, insult or jokes, because if that was the case, he would have banned the name of Muhammad from being given to any other person. Let's be honest, there have been a whole lot of people given the name of Muhammad that have been bad, and I mean really bad. So bad that their behavior was dishonoring or insulting to the prophet that carried the name before them; and as it is said, actions speak louder than words. So, it is hypocritical for people to kill in the name of the prophet's honor in one area (pictures or cartoons) but find no issue with it in another (name sakes behavior).

From the time of the prophet's death, people have been using his name, with some being bad kids and then bad grownups, and nobody ever killed them for this behavior. So, this shows that this is a man-made hysteria with the advent of media. Furthermore, I propose that there was some MAN that came along wanting some new followers and found a way that he could use this issue to create some divide in the world of religions, all while getting some people that were looking for a fresh new something to react to, and now it has stuck.

Thus, I say that through the writing in the Quran, and through the historical practices of the Middle-East, specifically the Muslims in being okay with the behavior of kids/men with the name of Muhammad and the act of killing people in the name of Muhammad to protect his honor, is in reality murder by Islamic law as well as anyone else's law. In reality, those that are doing these killings are in actuality dishonoring and/or insulting the prophet by this behavior. The actual act of killing/murdering someone is far worse or dishonoring of the Prophet Muhammad than any comic or cartoon could ever be.

Islam is the fastest growing religion at this time and I cannot figure out why. With the outward message of concur, submit, or die, who in the world would want to live like that? It seems that there is a part of the human nature that shows that some people want to be in control, while others are in a need of being controlled. This makes no sense to me, as I inject another life story;

Once I was with these two people, one asked me if I was a leader or a follower.

I replied, "I am neither."

He said, "Oh yes you must be one or the other."

I again replied, "No, I really am neither."

The other guy then spoke up and said, "You are a leader, I have been around you a while and I can say for sure, you are a leader."

I then replied, "No I am not. I am not a follower or a leader. I really will not follow anyone when I can think for myself. And if anyone is following me it is not because I am a leader it is because they are lost."

But, I will say this, if I was to be in a group, I could not be in one that said we want everyone to think and live all the same way or we are going to kill them. That would be a horrible life, everybody all the same? That would not be good. Besides, this is a religion we are talking about, a religion that on the first page of the main book, the Quran, it says there are indeed some people that just won't be working with this program and for those people God will handle them.

However, I did notice this book is filled with reference or rules that say time after time that men are in charge and the women are to be submissive to the man. So, I wonder, is this religion becoming so popular here in the USA because of the advent of the women's rights? Is it so popular because of our racial divide? Is it because, this religion is not the Christianity that was forced upon the black community before the equal rights? Are some people joining just because they want something that is not what they consider the white mans' religion? Are some people joining because they know once they get a Muslim woman they can go back to the "good old days" of having her barefoot and in the kitchen with no backtalk? I don't know on this, but I do know for sure I cannot see how so many people here in the USA are willfully joining. While in other regions of the world Islamic groups are banding together and forcing people to join or die, because they are running out of willful volunteers. More and more people the world over are becoming literate, and with this increased literacy will come more and more people that are smart enough to see that this volatile religion needs some changes...

I know the ISIS group over in the middle-east right now is boasting how they feel life should be, like it was back in the 10th to 16th century, but yet, they have no problem using modern guns, bombs, cars, internet and all those modern 15th century devices, (I say while shaking my head in wonderment). As well, they are killing people in the name of advancing their religion as being the right way things are supposed to be. Yet, they are always wearing masks. Why? If this is the right way why are you hiding behind the mask? Are they ashamed of something? Are they ashamed of what they are doing? Are they ashamed of being right?

Time for another little story.

There was a Rabbi on his deathbed. Two men came to see him. They asked him for one last blessing.

He replied, "Surely, may you fear god's eyes as much as you fear man's eyes."

They looked at him and said, "Rabbi, there must be more, what does that mean."

The Rabbi replied, "You commit crimes and hope that no man will see you. Yet God's eyes see everything and yet you do not care."

With that I again ask, why do they wear masks?

If this religion truly has a god that wants you to kill people why would anyone want to be in that religion? I say this because ISIS and other Islamic extremist groups that are doing this are also professing that there will be a judgment day, (which the Quran does state). Well, if this God is so blood thirsty for you to kill in this life, what makes you think he won't be the one doing the killing in the next life? I am not sure this would be the god I would be looking forward to meeting. However a counter point on whether the Islamic god is really this hostile, violent, or blood thirsty, in an example from a Hadith Qudsi is the hadith of **Abu Hurairah** who said that Muhammad said:

*When God decreed the Creation He pledged Himself by writing in His book which is laid down with Him: My mercy prevails over My wrath, [Related by **al-Bukhari**, **Muslim**, **an-Nasa'i** and **Ibn Majah**.]*

With this being a quote from the Prophet Muhammad that so many people are killing for to protect his honor, I think they are missing some, if not most, of the points both Muhammad and God were trying to make on how to live your life. Here, it states that God's mercy prevails over His wrath, for those Muslims that are doing the killings - this means He (God) sides with the less violent actions.

There is only one way to stop the Islamic War on Terror, that stop must come from within.

All the Islamic leaders the world over must address this issue. All the Muslim leaders must publicly, as well as in the Masques, denounce this practice of this bloodshed.

. Furthermore, the practicing men and women of Islam must also speak up and make their voices heard, denouncing these violent practices. As long as the Muslim population as a whole stays quite the bloodshed will continue. When the people of the religion say nothing, their silence, for whatever reason is in reality endorsing the behavior. This is a time when it needs to be said, and understood, that;

Those people that do or say nothing to stop these violent bloody acts are ultimately just as guilty of committing the acts themselves.

Islam, like Judaism and Christianity, though it is the youngest of the three has endured a split into two factions as well. However, the difference with the Islamic split is twofold; one the split happened within 25 years of its birth. This split developed as soon as Muhammad died without naming a successor or explaining the process on how to determine the transition process of Islamic leaders would come to be. The second difference is, the split between the Islamic sects is a violent one. The two sects Sunnis and Shiites have actually been fighting (to the death in many cases) from the time of Muhammad's death; again this makes no sense to me, and without question this is not healthy.

However this could be the very key to making things better. The fact that the two Muslim sects fight between themselves makes it understandable why they strike out at others. It is not until the two sects make a bridge between them that they will be able to accept non-Muslims as not being a threat. The key here is finding a strong Islamic Imam that can start this bridge; the cornerstone can and should be the fact that both sects are rooted in the same book. There has to be an understanding that fighting and or killing is not the way. The Jews and the Christians are at peace within their divisions which allows them the inner strength to be at peace with others.

Bring this back to the issue of making cartoons of Muhammad; I know the Jewish faith doesn't go a day without being the punch line of a joke to someone. Christianity as well is okay with jokes. Here is a couple;

This is a description of a cartoon about the Jewish world.

Moses is standing on the side of a hill; several people are looking at him. One says – "Forty years wondering in the desert, - could you find a god that knew a short cut."

Another on,

A little boy is in the living room looking at his grandmother sitting in her chair. The boy asks her – "Why did Mosses wonder in the desert for forty years?"

His grandmother responds – "Because even back then men would not stop and ask for directions."

See now these are funny. Here is one for Christianity.

There is an elderly couple in their sixties standing in their kitchen when a voice from nowhere says you get one free prayer to ask for anything you want.

The wife makes her prayer; she says, she prays for plane tickets to see the world. Poof a cloud of smoke clears and there on the table is a stack of plane tickets to places around the world.

The man then gets all happy and he makes his free prayer; he says – "I want a wife thirty years younger than me." Poof the smoke clears and he looks at his wife, she looks the same, he goes to the mirror and sees that he is now ninety.

These are funny shots are religion, when people are strong enough and confident enough in who they are, they can make jokes like this and not end up feeling they need to kill someone. It is a shame that Islam as a whole is missing out on this part of life. Humor is not only a good thing; it is a gift from God himself. If you do not believe me, just take some time to look around you. He created humans didn't he? Now that shows God has a sense of humor.

As I have said, religion on the surface is good, and when blended with the right amount of the underlying meaning, can be great. However, I have also said that sometimes men can and do misinterpret the message of religion and turn it into a weapon, a weapon that can at times be used to hurt people and even destroy all of civilization. Here, to me it is the people of Islam that have misinterpreted so much of the writing's and messages of the Islamic books. I prime example here is, as I have previously stated it was written; that It is said that the Torah is true but men have distorted the words and meaning of the Torah. Now here we are fifteen hundred years later and I bring that question back to the Imams of Islam. Is it that the Quran is true but the men have distorted it?

I say that because the following it true, the people of Islam make it clear that they want to kill all Jews. My question is why? The Quran does not call for that, in contrast the Quran says that you are to love all people of the "Book" or "Believers." I cannot find any justification for this behavior in the Quran. The Torah is the root of the Quran thus the Jewish people should be embraced with love rather than targeted for death.

Furthermore, this practice is not new, history is filled with times and societies in which the Jewish people were classified as second class citizens for no other reason than being Jewish. Which has always baffled me, much like the chaplain I encountered that said to me "There is nothing in the Jewish faith that belongs in his chapel, I have to wonder why this is; is it out of fear? If so, fear of what? My thinking is it is more out of lack of understanding. With that being the case I would like to share just a little on the Jewish spiritual practices.

As I said earlier we read from the Torah, most commonly known as the "Old Testament. The Torah is broken down into sections or portions starting with Genesis and ending with Deuteronomy. The book is sectioned out like this so people can read a "portion" a week thus being able to keep up with the Bible without being overwhelmed or intimidated by it massiveness. This portions are then set to a weekly schedule starting with Genesis 1;1 during the week of Rosh Ha Shanna and ending the reading schedule with Deuteronomy the week before Rosh Ha Shanna a year later. We then start all over again, doing this same practice every year, thus we end up reading the Torah all the way through every year. We don't get to skip from one good exciting part to another, we are stuck having to read every bit of it every year even the dull and boring sections of Leviticus. This practice and schedule is done by ever Jewish person in every Temple and Synagogue the world over. This way whenever any Jewish person is traveling they can go to any Temple or Synagogue and feel at home. However, I will say just because the people are all reading the same Torah portion does not mean they have the same customs. On the contrary, the customs differ from Temple to Temple let along city to city or state to state, not to mention from country to country.

However, while the customs may differ the message will always remain the same. The following are a couple of recitations that are said during a Jewish Sabbath service;

Oh God, may we never become complacent, faltering in our effort to build a world of peace.

Let the nations know and understand that justice and right are better than dominion and conquest;

May all come to see that it is not by might nor by power but by Your spirit that life prevails.

Also;

Grant us peace. Your most precious gift,

O Eternal Source of peace.

And give us the will to proclaim its message

to all the peoples of the earth.

Bless our country as a safeguard of peace,

Its advocate among the nations.

May contentment reign within our borders,

health and happiness within our homes.

Strengthen the bonds of friendship and fellowship among all the inhabitants of every land.

Plant virtue in every sole, and may the love of Your Name hallow every homeand every heart.

Blessed are You, Eternal One who blesses our people with peace.

These recitations are ones of peace and love. Peace and love not just for the Jewish people but for all the people of the world. We as Jews do not pray for war, we do not pray for hate, we do not pray for any other person to fail or fall on hard times, we pray for all people, or all walks of life, religious or not to be happy, healthy and successful. It is for these reasons that I cannot understand the hatred bestowed on the Jewish people by the Islamic faith. So I ask all my Muslim friends as well as all that don't know me, to look at your book, look at the writings and see that there in fact is no directive to hate or kill anyone let along the Jewish people. People do not have to hate other people just because that is how it has always been.

My final thought on this issue of religious fighting. I had a friend tell me one time that the best way to look at people in life is; treat everyone as you would treat God, because you never know if that person is the Messiah!

As I am nearing the close on this chapter of religion, let me take some time to share a couple of my personal thoughts on some commonly asked topics I am asked. '

On the statement that tomorrow is promised to no one, so live today as if it were your last.

> In the text when it states that tomorrow is promised to no one, it does not mean the day after today. It is the spiritual reference to the next lifetime. And when it says that you are to live everyday as if it were your last; this

does not mean go spend every dime you have because you will not be needing a savings account. This too is a spiritual reference to making sure you are doing all the right things so you won't have any "unfinished business" if your were to die a sudden unexpected death leaving you no chance to make amends for any wrong doings you may have done.

This point, will tie well into my next point, that being that the Jewish text that says if you live by the law, you shall surely live forever but if you don't live by the law, you shall surely die. While that sounds a bit harsh, it really is not. Many Christians ask me how Jewish people get around this. First I tell them, simple, we live by the law. Then, I take the time to explain it as follows;

The true meaning of this is as follows; this is not about you and your physical body, this is all about you and your life. If you live by the law, you shall surely live forever means that if you do right by people in your life and truly make a difference in a positive way you will live forever. Meaning, even after you die people will not only remember you but still continue to do the things you did or wanted to have done. Examples include

President Lincoln, Martin Luther King Jr and even my Uncle you call Jesus. You see these people all made a difference for the better; they lived by the law, that law being, treat other people the way they should be treated. As you can see, they are not physically alive but yet they still live through the positive changes they made to humanity. Now this does not have to be on a scale that large. In fact, in almost all cases it is not. Simply being a good parent, good teacher, a good role model to people in the community does the same thing, if not more. Think about the good father point, the amount of positive influence a father or mother can have on a child is infinite. How many generations a parent's teachings can affect are equally infinite. A good parent, like a good teacher, can make the whole difference in a child's life for the better.

Thus, a parent or any other person that walks the walk as well as talks the talk, as Jesus would, will surely live forever.

For my thought on the Messiah

I am not a person that believes that there will be a messiah that comes and there will be one big judgment day for the whole planet. No, I see it a bit different; I see things like this. Each and every day is a judgment day for someone. Yes every day someone passes and at that time it is their judgment day, I also see each person having their own individual judgment day I also see each person having their own individual messiah experience. What I mean by this is, that I believe that each and every person will have some event or experience in their life that will cause them to see life in a different way. This will be something that will really shake them up; it will be something that will give them a reason to re-evaluate how they are living and whether or not it is time to make a change.

Then, from that point on, if they chose the right option, life will be all good. As the book says, after the coming of the messiah life will be all good. Well, for that person, that will be the case. Now the next door neighbor might still have some issues, but they will not affect him/her because they have made the change.

I am saying that each person's messiah experience as well their judgment day experience is all their own just like their relationship with God. In the book of Exodus chapter 3, Moses has his first encounter with the talking burning bush. At this time while Moses is talking to the burning bush, the bush is telling Moses he is really talking to God. Moses says, "Ok well if you are God and you want me to go back to Egypt to ask them to let all their free labor people leave with me, just who should I tell them sent me?" In the Hebrew text there are three words that are translated differently by different people, but one of the translations says, "I am who I am." This says, that God is telling Moses, "That you tell them that I am God, and that to each and every person I have my own relationship so no specific name will suffice."

It is along this line that I say is the same with the Messiah experience as well as the judgment day experience. Each person will have their own personal experience. Since this Hebrew text was written as an account of the very first conversation with Moses and we have established that each of the big three religions are of the same God of Abraham, it is clear to me that this message applies to all people. So therefore, I believe that all people can have their own personal relationship with God. It does not matter which religion you are riding with.

However, in my life, I have learned that not all people see things the way I do. For example here are a couple of exchanges I had with a chaplain a couple of years back.

> On one of my first encounters with this man, he was asking me why I was Jewish and why I had not converted to Christianity, the true religion as he told me.
>
> My response was that I was okay with being Jewish, as well I was okay with him, and others being, Christian or whatever.
>
> He did not take that very well and thought I was not very serious about God.
>
> I said to him at that point, 'Well to me, it is all the same. We are all trying to get to the same place. You take Third Street to get to the ballpark and I take Seventh Street, does not matter as long as we all get there."
>
> He replied, "Well that's fine if you think God is a ballpark."
>
> I shook my head and said to him, "Well I can see we can't talk parables with you."

On another occasion I went to see this chaplain;

I asked him what he had at the chapel for the Jewish faith.

His response was; there is nothing in the Jewish faith that belongs in this chapel.

I just smiled and asked him if he was serious.

He refused to talk to me after that.

As I say, religion is not bad; it is the people that make religion go badly. On that tip I have also shown how people are taking religion into the political realm and how it is affecting (infecting) our politics right here in the USA. I truly think and feel that religion is a very important and needed aspect of not only our lives here in the United States, but indeed for all of humanity. However, looking right here, today, in the United States with a very high literacy rate, we are still seeing some religious extremists trying to make an impact. This is why I started this book with the Pledge of Allegiance and finished with Religion. They are my two favorite issues. Again, Ben Carson is right when he said that we cannot have a person(s) in power that will put their religious principles before those of the Constitution and Bill of Rights.

A prime example of what can happen if we allow for religion to have an uncontested influence on our governmental decisions, are the events that occurred in Malaysia, June of 2015. In this case Malaysia had an incident where they brought manslaughter charges against some tourists that had taken some nude photos. The charges were grounded in the argument that the tourists angered the gods when they took these photos and the god's response was to cause the mountain to quake, and this quake caused rock slides that killed 18 people. It is for this reason that we need to have concerns with the way we allow religion to affect our governmental decisions.

Here is an off the wall thought about religion;

I hear people all the time talking about a loved one that has passed on, looking down on them and guiding their way. Now honestly, do we all really think that people die and go to heaven, and then are watching over us?

- I mean, please, if we really thought that, why would we continue to do some of the things we do?
- If you really notice, almost every person that lives a "wild" or "criminal" life will be the one(s) that speak those words. Makes you want to say "HUM!"
- Plus, none of us would ever have a sex life! Please, not while our loved ones are watching!

The following is another story;

> I was taking a communications class when the topic came up on the importance of having forgiveness in communication when talking to others. The point was that if a person has said something that has offended you, you must be able to forgive them if there is any hope for having a productive conversation. At this point, the instructor asked the class for feedback as to how we felt about this. (At this point let me say, in this class, we had several people that had known each other for several years.)

A man I will refer to as "Mark" spoke up first and said, "I am a Christian and in my faith we are required to always give forgiveness because that is what Jesus died for."

At this point the instructor asked for other views, as we all know in most classrooms the students are almost always reluctant to vocally participate. With no input coming, a man named "Mac" spoke up and introduced himself as a well learned and practicing Muslim. He went on to speak on the subject from the Islamic view, he stated, "While Muslims are not required to automatically forgive a person, it is accepted that it is always in the best interest of humanity to forgive and move on."

The instructor then assessed that from those two religious viewpoints, we should all have some very healthy and forgiving conversations. She then asked for other views, and again there were no voluntary participants. With no persons speaking up, class members started looking at me to add to the mix. I say this because it was common knowledge that I was Jewish and they were looking for me to render a view from the Jewish perspective.

At which I told them, "No, they would not want to know my view." After a little harassment I agreed to give them my view. It was short, simple and to the point.

I explained that from my view on things from my Jewish teachings, there would be no forgiveness.

As you might expect, that created quite an emotional response. After a few seconds of grumbling from all my classmates, I asked if they would like an explanation.

I then went on to explain that in order for a person to have to forgive another, that person must first condemn the other, and in order to condemn you must be in a position to judge a person, and in order to judge a person you must be in a position above them. However, in my world, I was taught that all people are equal; meaning that I am no better than or no less than anyone else. In other words, I am in no position to judge anyone. Therefore, if I cannot judge, I cannot condemn, and if I cannot condemn, then there is no forgiveness to grant.

When I finished, Mac the Islamic speaker spoke up and said, "I have known this man for almost ten years, and he is telling the truth, that is exactly how he is."

My last story I promise.

During the spring of 2015, I was honored to have been invited to attend a baptism with my friends of the Mormon faith. It was during this ceremony that I heard the best Christian message ever. The man giving the sermon said;

"Jesus may have taken our sins away, but he left us with a life of responsibilities."

This my friends is the perfect way to close my chapter on religion.

Chapter 14

My closing thoughts

This book started with the pledge, continued through some political issues that were marred with religious strings. These strings are causing people to lose focus on not only the issues, but also the solutions. The problem I see with this is, these strings are injecting religion into our government rules and rulings. As I said in my opening, I am a man with very strong religious beliefs and convictions. However, I am also a very strong and proud American citizen that believes wholeheartedly in our Constitution and Bill of Rights. I believe so strongly in these that I am firm when I say, if we first stand and live by the rights and freedoms granted by the U.S. Constitution and Bill of Rights, we will always be allowed to be different yet still equal to every other citizen no matter who they are, what they do, or what they look like. We can do all this and still be able to maintain our religious beliefs and practices no matter what they may or may not be. We are but one Nation, indivisible with liberty and justice for all.

On the other hand, if we all put our religious practices and beliefs first and the Constitution second, we will inevitably be fighting over these very practices and beliefs. Because once we open the door to let religion take top billing, we will get into a never ending blood bath as to which religion or practices we are to follow. If world history has taught us nothing else, it should have taught us that. None of the religions can agree amongst themselves as it is now, look at each of the three; The Jews now have three categories, the Christians have countless denominations and Islam split into two practices shortly after Muhammad passed away. We see how each of these religions has conflicting policies and practices within themselves as well as serious conflicts with the others. Why in the world would any of us think, we as a whole would or could manage to agree on which religion and or which religious practices and policies would dictate how our countries policies, practices and laws would be implemented?

As a man that truly believes in the existence of a God I have to say the bottom line is; religion does not give, grant or promote freedom, on the contrary religion creates division. Our Constitution gives us freedoms and rights, as well it gives us all an equal common ground to start with and finish with, for we are all Americans first, and then we are free to be any type of subsection of our society we want to be.

We are always Americans first!

What is the Purpose of Life

What I see as the purpose of life is; for each person to live a life, grow old and sit on their front porch sipping on their tea looking back on their lives and have more smiles then they do frowns.

Again I Thank you for purchasing this book and I hope you enjoy your read. Once you have finished I also encourage you to visit the web page; BooksBySDOwens.com to write a review. I look forward to hearing your views. Note; you may have to type the web address into the address bar to assure reaching the web page.

I would also like to make note that for every book sold we will donate fifty cents to the American Alzheimer's Association